WOMEN IN BLACK

The Creepy Companions of the Mysterious M.I.B.

Published by Lisa Hagan Books 2016

Powered by

SHADOW
TEAMS

Copyright © Nick Redfern.

ISBN: 9780996968683

Cover design and interior layout by Simon Hartshorne

WOMEN IN BLACK

The Creepy Companions of the Mysterious M.I.B.

NICK REDFERN

Contents

Introduction

Within the world of UFO research, the Men in Black are about as legendary as they are feared. These pale-faced, ghoulish entities have for decades terrorized into silence both witnesses to, and researchers of, UFO encounters. Theories about who or what the MIB might be are legion. They include: extraterrestrials, government agents, demonic creatures, vampires, time-travelers from the future, and inter-dimensional beings from realms that co-exist with ours. There may very well be more than one explanation for the unsettling phenomenon.

While much has been written on the sinister and occasionally deadly actions of the MIB, very little has been penned on the subject of their equally bone-chilling companions: the *Women* in Black. Make no mistake: the WIB are all too real. And they are as ominous, predatory and dangerous as their male counterparts. In the same way that the Men in Black don't always wear black, but sometimes wear military uniforms or specifically beige-colored outfits, so do the WIB, who are also quite partial to white costumes. In that sense, "WIB" is, just like "MIB," a term that is somewhat flexible in terms of actual nature and description.

The WIB may not have achieved the iconic status of the MIB – *until now* - but these fearsome females, and their collective role in silencing those that immerse themselves in the UFO puzzle, as well as in the domains of the occult and the world of the paranormal, are all too terrifyingly real. Not only that: the WIB have a long and twisted history.

Years before they plagued and tormented flying saucer seekers, the Women in Black roamed the landscape by night, stealing babies and young children, and plaguing the good folk of 19th century United States and United Kingdom. They were also up to their infernal tricks in the 1920s.

A definitive WIB surfaced in nothing less than a piece of publicity-based footage for a Charlie Chaplin movie, *The Circus*, which was made in 1928. The footage, undeniably genuine and shown not to have been tampered with, reveals what appears to be an old, short lady, wearing a long black coat and a black hat pulled low over her face, while walking through Los Angeles in West Coast heat. If that was not strange enough, she is clearly holding to her ear what appears to be a cell-phone and is talking into it as she walks. Weirder still, the Woman in Black sports an enormous pair of black shoes, which look most out of place, given her short stature. She also seems to be taking careful steps to avoid her face being seen clearly. Might she have been some kind of time-traveling Woman in Black, working hard – but spectacularly failing – to blend in with the people of Los Angeles, all those years ago?

Fifteen years later, a terrifying WIB haunted the Bender family of Bridgeport, Connecticut. It so happens that a certain Albert Bender, of that very clan, near-singlehandedly began the Men in Black mystery. In the early 1950s, Bender, after establishing the *International Flying Saucer Bureau*, was visited and threatened with nothing less than death by a trio of pale, skinny, fedora-wearing MIB. They were visits that firmly set the scene for the decades of MIB-themed horror and mayhem that followed. Bender's visitors were not secret agents of government, however. He said they materialized in his bedroom – a converted attic in a creepy old house of *Psycho* proportions - amid an overpowering stench of sulfur. They were shadowy beings with demon-like, glowing eyes. We surely cannot blame the CIA, the FBI, or even the all-powerful NSA, for that!

In 1956, UFO sleuth Gray Barker penned a book on Bender's confrontations with the Men in Black. It was titled *They Knew Too Much About Flying Saucers* and became a classic. Six years later, Bender penned his very own book on his encounters with the MIB: *Flying Saucers and the Three Men*. It was these two books that brought the MIB into the minds and homes of flying saucer enthusiasts across the world. After which, Bender dropped each and every one of his ties to Ufology. He was careful to avoid speaking about the subject ever again, and, thereon, focused his time on running the appreciation-society of composer Max Steiner.

Back in the 1930s, however, the Bender family had a black-garbed woman in its midst that tormented both young and old in the dead of night. Predating Albert Bender's own experience with the MIB by years, the hideous silencer in black haunted the Benders near-endlessly. For the Bender family, long before the MIB there was a Woman in Black.

In the 1960s, the emotionless, evil-eyed WIB turned up in the small, doom-filled town of Point Pleasant, West Virginia. And right around the time that sightings of the legendary flying monster known as Mothman were at their height. Claiming to be "census-takers," these pale-faced, staring-eyed WIB practically forced their way into the homes of frightened witnesses to Mothman. What began as seemingly normal questions about the number of people in the house, of the average income of the family, and of the number of rooms in the relevant property, soon mutated into something much stranger: persistent and intrusive questions about strange dreams, about unusual telephone interference, and about beliefs regarding the world of all-things of a paranormal nature soon followed.

One of the WIB that put in an appearance at Point Pleasant claimed to have been the secretary of acclaimed author on all-things paranormal, John Keel, author of *The Mothman Prophecies*. Just like her male counterparts, she turned up on doorsteps late at night, waiting to be invited in, before grilling mystified and scared souls about their UFO and Mothman encounters. Then vanishing into the night after carefully instilling feelings of distinct fear in the interviewees. Only when dozens of such stories got back to Keel did he realize the sheer, incredible, scale of the dark ruse that was afoot. Keel had to break the unsettling news to each and every one of the frightened souls who contacted him: *"I have no secretary."*

Mothman: Point Pleasant, West Virginia's legendary, flying monster. (Nick Redfern, 2014).

In the 1970s, wig-wearing and anemic-looking WIB made life hell for more than a few people who were unfortunate enough to cross their paths. Something similar occurred in England, Scotland, and Ireland during the 1980s: a weird wave of encounters with "phantom social-workers" hit the UK. They were out of the blue encounters that eerily paralleled the incidents involving WIB-based "census-takers" that manifested in West Virginia back in the 1960s.

Just as menacing, sinister and unsettling as their American cousins, these particular WIB began by claiming that reports had reached them of physical abuse to children in the family home which had to be investigated. Worried parents, clearly realizing that these hag-like crones were anything but social-workers, invariably phoned the police. The WIB, realizing when they had been rumbled, made hasty exits and always before law-enforcement personnel were on the scene. Most disturbing of all, there was a near-unanimous belief on the part of the parents that the Women in Black were intent on kidnapping the children for purposes unknown, but surely no good.

Back to the United States, in early 1987, Bruce Lee, a book-editor for Morrow, had an experience with a WIB-type character in an uptown New York bookstore. Lee's attention to the curious woman – short, wrapped in a wool hat and a long scarf, and wearing large black sunglasses behind which could be seen huge, "mad dog" eyes – was prompted by something strange and synchronistic. She and her odd partner were speed-reading the pages of the then-newly-published UFO-themed book, *Communion*, by Whitley Strieber. It was a book published by the very company Lee was working for. Lee quickly exited the store, shaken to the core by the appearance and hostile air that the peculiar pair oozed in his presence.

In 2001, Colin Perks, a British man obsessed with finding the final resting place of King Arthur, received a nighttime visit from a beautiful but emotionless Woman in Black; one with near-milk-white skin. She claimed to represent a secret arm of the British Government that was intent on shutting down research into all realms of the paranormal. When Perks defiantly and defensively said he would not be stopped by veiled threats, the Woman in Black responded with a slight, emotion-free smile and advised him he had just made a big mistake and that he should soon expect another visitor. That other visitor soon turned up, late one dark night. It was a hideous, gargoyle-like beast with fiery, blazing red eyes that loomed large over Perks' bed in the early hours. Perks, forever thereafter blighted by fear and paranoia, came to believe his Woman in Black and the winged beast were one and the same: namely, a monstrous shape-shifter, a nightmarish thing intent on scaring him from continuing his dedicated research.

Both 2012 and 2014 saw incredible and frightening encounters with the Women in Black across the United States. And, as you will now learn, the above-accounts amount to the mere tip of what is a gigantic, much under-appreciated iceberg.

When paranormal activity occurs, when UFOs intrude upon the lives of petrified people, and when researchers of all things paranormal get too close to the truth for their own good, the WIB are ready to strike. They dwell within darkness, they surface when the landscape is black and shadowy, and they spread terror and negativity wherever they walk. Or, on occasion, silently *glide*. They are the Women in Black. Fear them. Keep away from them. And never, *ever*, let them in.

1

"He saw a lady in black in his bedroom at night"

Albert Bender, as I noted in the Introduction to this book, is inextricably linked to the enigma of the *Men* in Black. For that very reason alone, it's decidedly unusual that practically everyone in the UFO community who has ever commented on Bender's encounters with the dark-suited ones has overlooked something massively important. We're talking about his family's links to…a *Woman* in Black. She was a foul and spectral crone who was obsessed with nothing less than coins. Bender, meanwhile, and as will soon become apparent, had an obsession with alchemy. This issue of a connection between coins, alchemy, Women in Black and Men in Black should not be ignored. It must be said, however, that nearly every UFO researcher who has studied the matter of the WIB and the MIB has done exactly that. It's time for the matter to be rectified.

Alchemy is the secret, fabled means by which base-metals, such as lead, can be turned into highly valuable metals, including silver and gold. In centuries past, alchemists toiled night and day to uncover the legendary secrets of the so-called Philosopher's Stone – the enigmatic substance that could supposedly allow for the priceless transformation to take place. And of particular fascination to both the WIB and the MIB, when it comes to alchemy, are coins and the means by which a fairly ordinary coin can be turned into something much more. Or even into something much less. As we will see in the chapters ahead, alchemy and mysterious, black-garbed visitors at the front-door are regular bedfellows. But, before we get to that, let's focus on Albert Bender. After all, what better place to start with a discussion of the Women in Black than with the man who made the Men in Black legendary?

"My cousin wore a coin on an unbroken chain around his neck constantly, even to bed"

In 1933, while he was just a young child, Bender's mother told him the spine-tingling story of a deeply malevolent family ghost. That of a Woman in Black. There were no friendly, fun, night-time tales for young Bender. The story revolved around a second-cousin of Bender's who, while only six years of age at the time, moved into a sinister old house with his family. It was a house that sat adjacent to an old, abandoned mine-shaft. The mine was a downright eerie place: it was filled with angular shadows and darkened passageways. Old wooden supports creaked and groaned endlessly, and a multitude of bats and rats called it their lair.

It was also a mine in which, years earlier, a despondent young woman slit her throat and, as the blood cascaded forth, threw herself into the depths of one of the darkened, old shafts. Her battered and torn body was finally recovered and taken into the house in where Bender's cousin lived, before being buried in the local graveyard. The woman, noted Bender, was said to have been a definitive witch, one that "lived alone with a great many cats" and who "was said to prowl about only at night." Bender added that: "My cousin wore a coin on an unbroken chain around his neck constantly, even to bed. After having lived in the house a few months, his parents noticed his health was failing. He would not eat, and claimed he saw a lady in black in his bedroom at night. Of course, they thought it all nonsense and that he was only dreaming, but soon they began to have sleepless nights when the boy would scream out in his sleep and they would find it necessary to go and comfort him."

In the early hours of one particularly fraught morning, Bender's cousin awoke the whole family; he was wailing like a veritable banshee. His parents raced to his room and noticed that the coin had been unhooked from the chain and was now positioned on the pillow.

According to Bender, the boy told his mother and father that, "the lady in black was trying to choke him and take his coin away from him."

The local doctor in town dismissed the boy's words with a wave of his hand, and said the entire thing was down to nightmares and nothing else. Very soon thereafter, the doctor would be proven catastrophically wrong.

With no end in sight to the boy's malignant night-terrors, both parents elected to sleep in their son's room, alongside him, until things finally calmed down and normality was hopefully restored. On the fourth night, they were woken up by the horrific sight of a hooded, female form - dressed completely in black, and with sickly-looking skin – that slowly and silently glided across the room, right in the direction of the boy. A bony hand moved slowly down to grasp the coin, at which point the boy's father jumped up, lit a candle, and firmly thrust it in the face of the WIB.

Bender said: "They could see a pale, chalky-white face staring at them."

In an instant the terrifying hag screamed at both parents; its wild and hostile eyes flashing quickly from father to mother and back again. Suddenly, it was gone – and so was the coin. Not surprisingly, the terrified family vacated the house within a week. The boy, to the relief of everyone concerned, quickly recovered.

And there is more, too.

A predatory encounter in the dead of night.
(Carmilla, D.H. Friston, 1872).

Albert Bender, a student of alchemy

John Keel, commenting on the Men in Black mystery, said that Albert Bender "explored" the domain of alchemy. Bender did far more than that: he was absolutely *obsessed* with the subject and its centuries-old secrets. Amongst Albert Bender's most cherished books was Mary Shelley's *Frankenstein*. UKEssays notes: "*Frankenstein*, the novel written by Mary Shelley, takes ideas found in literary texts, moments in time, and people and incorporates them into the novel to tell the framed narrative. Alchemy and the alchemists, although scarcely mentioned in the novel, are quintessential to the continuation of the plot. It is the alchemists and their ideas, particularly those of Paracelsus and the concept of the elixir of life that propel Victor Frankenstein to pursue the idea of creation through science, ultimately leading Victor to the creation of the creature in *Frankenstein*."

On closely related territory, Bender was particularly entranced by the literary work of Edgar Allan Poe; one of Bender's favorite of all authors. And, for Bender, a particular, stand-out story of Poe's was *The Gold Bug*. Barton Levi St. Armand, in an essay titled *Poe's "Sober Mystification,"* says: "Poe was cognizant of the implemental surface of alchemy, and as Burton Pollin has pointed out, he was at least familiar with Isaac D 'Israeli's note on 'Alchymy' in his 1834 *Curiosities of Literature*, which contained the provocative suggestion that 'Modern chemistry is not without a *hope*, not to say a *certainty*, of verifying the golden visions of the alchymists'. The tale that dilates on this idea and most bears out the fact of Poe's adeptness in the philosophy of alchemy is one which is usually taken as simply an ingenious mystery-adventure story, the intriguing 'Gold-Bug.'"

Another favorite story for Bender was H.P. Lovecraft's *The Alchemist*. It's a dark and twisted tale of a man, one Charles le Sorcier, who uncovers the secrets of the Philosopher's Stone and alchemy, and uses it to massively prolong his life. He does so as a means to kill each and every successive heir to the Antoine family castle when they reach the age of thirty-two. It was one Count Antoine – of that same family - who, centuries earlier, killed le Sorcier's father, a wizard named Michel Mauvais.

On top of that, Bender had an obsession with Bram Stoker's gothic fantasy, the acclaimed *Dracula*. Not only was Stoker, himself, deeply interested in alchemy, but, in the pages of his classic novel, so was the fictional, Transylvanian vampire count himself.

Thus, we see that, in reality, Albert Bender's exposure to the blackest mystery of all *did not* begin in the early 1950s, which was when he received a visit from three menacing MIB that rivaled anything ever written about by his hero, Edgar Allan Poe. The reality of the situation is that it all began two decades earlier, in the 1930s, and with a Woman in Black, one who had a thing for coins, and for making them disappear, too.

There is another issue too. You will recall that, according to the legend, the Woman in Black who haunted the Bender family "lived alone with a great many cats." In a strange fashion, so did Albert Bender. At the height of his UFO research in the early 1950s, the solitary, unmarried, girlfriendless Bender converted his attic-based abode into what he proudly called his "chamber of horrors." It was a room filled with all manner of gruesome paintings of demonic entities, monsters, and human skulls. An "altar" to the underworld was constructed as Bender sought ways to contact the very darkest things lurking and prowling on the "other side." And, he adorned a portion of one of the walls with no less than ten paintings of large black cats, all with staring, hypnotic eyes.

While, today, admittedly, we are forced to speculate, it seems likely that (A) being conversant with tales of both the Women in Black and the MIB; (B) having an awareness of the WIB connection to the transmutation of coins; (C) possessing a keen knowledge of alchemy; and (D) obsessing over black cats, Albert Bender very likely knew *far* more about this menacing, black-shrouded mystery woman that plagued his family than has previously been suspected or realized.

2

"They are surely the saucer people you told us about"

Truman Bethurum was a Californian, born in 1898, who spent much of his early years working jobs that never seemed to last. His first marriage both began and crumbled during the Second World War. He entered into a second marriage only several months after the war ended, and ultimately wound up working out in the harsh, hot deserts of Nevada – specifically in the highway construction game. It was while Bethurum was out in the desert, in 1952, and while his second wife, Mary, was stuck at home in Santa Barbara, that Bethurum claimed he had an extremely close encounter with extraterrestrials on Mormon Mesa, a near-2000-foot-high foot high mount in Nevada's Moapa Valley.

On the fateful night in question, and after the working day was over, Bethurum climbed the mountain, primarily to search for shells, something that Mary particularly enjoyed collecting. The story goes that Bethurum was rendered into a strange, altered state of mind, during which aliens from another world suddenly manifested before him;

having arrived in a huge, gleaming, flying saucer that quietly descended to the desert floor. Although only around
four-feet-five to five-feet in height, the aliens were eerily
human-looking and claimed to come from a faraway planet
called Clarion. Not only that, their leader was one Captain Aura Rhanes, a shapely woman that the near-salivat-
ing Bethurum described as being "tops in shapeliness and
beauty." All thoughts of Mary – back in Santa Barbara –
were suddenly gone from Bethurum's mind.

Bethurum's odd story continued and grew at a steady
and controversial pace, as did his relationship to the flirty
Captain Rhanes. For months, Bethurum and Rhanes had
clandestine meetings; usually, late at night. They generally
occurred in isolated desert locations in Nevada, where,
after Rhanes' huge ship landed, the pair had long and deep
conversations about the state of the Earth, the Cold War,
and the captain's home world - to which she promised to
take Bethurum, one day. While Bethurum did not explicitly say so, there are more than a few nuggets of data in
Bethurum's collective work that suggests on a couple of
occasions the pair had just about the closest and most intimate encounters, of all. It's hardly surprising, then, that
many students of Ufology outright dismiss Bethurum's
story as either a hoax, or a fantasy born out of Bethurum's
unhappiness with both wife number one and two (eventually, there would be wife number three). There is, however,
one particularly fascinating aspect of Bethurum's claimed

experiences that has a significant bearing upon the matter of the Women in Black.

"It's her, isn't it?"

On two occasions, Bethurum said, he encountered Aura Rhanes under circumstances very different to those that occurred out in the desert, with Rhanes' huge flying saucer and her crew of little men in view. These additional encounters saw Rhanes operating in what can only be termed disguise. In fact, in definitive Woman in Black mode. There was nothing flirty or friendly about these close encounters, however: they were downright hostile. The first occurred around 3:00 a.m. – a time when a wealth of supernatural activity typically occurs - one August 1952 morning. Bethurum and a work friend, Whitey, had just finished their shift and decided to head off in Whitey's pick-up truck to a favorite, all-night diner in Glendale, Nevada. Whitey was someone who Bethurum had quietly confided in about his experiences with Aura Rhanes. He was also someone who, although fascinated by Bethurum's claims, was somewhat skeptical of the story. That is, until they entered the diner. Any skepticism Whitey had was very soon to be wiped out.

As the pair sat and drank coffee and ate pie, a noticeably quiet Whitey elbowed Bethurum in the ribs and motioned him to take a look at the end of the counter. Bethurum looked up. He was amazed and shocked to see Aura Rhanes, and an equally small male individual, standing there.

"It's her, isn't it?" asked Whitey. Bethurum nodded, pretty much in a state of near-shock. Both men watched carefully as Rhanes and her colleague took seats at a window table. In stark contrast to everyone else in the diner, Rhanes was dressed in black: black beret, wraparound black sunglasses, black velvet blouse, and black boots. The only thing that wasn't black: a "glaring red" skirt.

A worried Whitey asked: "What are you going to do?" Bethurum knew *exactly* what he was going to do. He composed himself, and walked over to talk to them. Whitey, however, was having none of it. He quickly exited the diner, preferring to sit in his truck, in the overwhelming darkness of the desert, rather than confront creatures from another world.

Perhaps trying to be a gentleman and tactful at the same time, Bethurum asked: "I beg your pardon, lady, but haven't we met before?"

Rhanes slowly looked up, glared at Bethurum with a wide-eyed and hostile stare, and uttered just one word: "*No.*" In private correspondence with fellow contactee, George Hunt Williamson, Bethurum said that Rhanes' "no" was uttered in a chilling, demonic tone. Almost like a "deadly hiss," to use Bethurum's own words.

Bethurum wasn't taking that for an answer: "You very closely resemble a lady I met some time ago out on Mormon Mesa."

The only response was another "*No*" of a very threatening style. Bethurum evidently didn't get the message. He blundered on with his line of questions. The answer was the same again and again. All the time, the weird little man with Rhanes – who also sported dark sunglasses - said not even a single word. Bethurum clearly recognized this odd behavior (or, rather, *non*-behavior) on the part of Rhanes' comrade: "The man did not give a hint that he either heard me or was even aware of my presence. He could have passed as a blind [and] deaf mute."

"The lady has on dark glasses and the man had a scar on his face"

As Bethurum walked away, and back to his table, the waitress came over – she just happened to be someone else that Bethurum had told of his otherworldly experiences. She said to him: "They are surely the saucer people you told us about."

He replied: "I thought so, too. But it may not be. The lady has on dark glasses and the man had a scar on his face."

The waitress gave a strange response: "I noticed that too, but it is not a scar. It is only penciled on."

With that, the odd little man motioned for the check. In a few moments, it was paid and the pair headed for the door. The waitress raced over to Bethurum and said: "The lady told me to tell you that she knows you, and that she was sorry and 'yes' is the answer to some of your questions."

It was then that something very strange happened, as Bethurum noted: "I saw them only a step from the door, before I turned to pay my check. When I turned back they were gone. I rushed outside, and there stood Whitey puffing nonchalantly on his cigarette."

When a dumbfounded Bethurum asked where the pair was, Whitey replied: "They never came out. Honest, Tru; not a blessed soul passed through that door until you came out."

Things were not over, however.

"Lady! Lady!"

Just a couple of weeks later, on a Saturday afternoon, Bethurum was having his hair trimmed at a barber's shop in Las Vegas, when he caught sight of Aura Rhanes, yet again. This time, she was walking along the sidewalk outside the barber's – wearing her same outfit of black sunglasses, black beret, black blouse, and red skirt. Bethurum practically threw his dollars and coins at the astonished barber and raced out of the door.

"Lady! Lady!" cried Bethurum, as he caught sight of Rhanes, about sixty feet ahead of him. She quickly turned, looked *directly* at him – despite the fact that the street was crowded and the shout could have come from any number of dozens of people on the sidewalk. She slowly shook her head. The stone-cold look on her face was one of pure evil. Bethurum got the message, as Rhanes vanished into the crowd. Nevertheless, it wasn't long before the nighttime liaisons in the desert were renewed – something that continued until November 2, 1952, when the little people of Clarion finally said their goodbyes. A crushed Bethurum was never to see his beautiful woman from the stars again. Maybe, as we've seen, that should be *sometimes* beautiful, but other times nothing but hostile.

Aura Rhanes: Truman Bethurum's mysterious woman from the stars (Carol Ann Rodriguez, 2016).

"Little people" is a very appropriate term to use, since there are clear and undeniable parallels between Aura Rhanes and the legendary female "fairy-folk" who would enchant men in Middle Ages-era Britain. The sexual aspects of such encounters, combined with notable amounts of missing time, make them the centuries-old mirror-images of today's alien abductions. Was Aura Rhanes a 20th century equivalent of a fairy-like "elemental?" Perhaps, yes.

Although the story of Truman Bethurum most assuredly stretches credibility to the max, it's important to note that it's filled with both WIB- and MIB-themed lore that simply was not in the public domain at the time in question, namely, the early years of the 1950s.

In the 1960s, a curious trend began in which the MIB regularly turned up to intimidate people in restaurants and diners – just as black-dressed Aura Rhanes did, way back in August 1952. The matter of Rhanes' sunglasses-wearing comrade having a painted-on scar mirrors the 1976 saga of a Dr. Herbert Hopkins, who's unsettling MIB seemed to be wearing lipstick, and whose story plays a key role in the saga of the Women in Black - as will become apparent later on in this book. Other WIB and MIB are often described as wearing make-up, as if to mask their milk-white, pasty skin.

Then there is the matter of the disappearance of the strange duo: as they exited the door of the diner, they vanished – as in literally. In no less than dozens of WIB and MIB cases, the black-clad fiends of the night seem to possess the unnerving ability to dematerialize as they exit the homes of those they terrorize. And, as we'll see later, there are other cases on record that mirror the experience of Bethurum in that old diner – and to a truly uncanny degree.

3

"We talked for hours about
traveling in space and time"

One of the strangest stories of the Women in Black comes
from a man named Brian Kinnersley. In the 1940s and 1950s,
Kinnersley's grandfather worked for the U.K.'s domestic
intelligence-gathering agency, MI5, which is the British
equivalent of the FBI. In 1955, Kinnersley's grandfather
was involved in a highly sensitive, top-secret investigation
of a man who claimed contact with a very human-looking
alien in the previous year, 1954. The reason why the affair
was considered so secret and sensitive was simple, yet also
fantastic and more than a little worrying. The man in question was a leading figure in the British military. He was
also someone who, at one point during the Cold War, had
his finger poised to push the dreaded "red button," had the
United Kingdom gone to war with the Soviets. His name
was Air Marshal Sir Beresford Peter Torrington Horsley.

Born in 1921, Horsley embarked upon an illustrious
career with the British military in 1939, when he took a
position as deck-boy on the *TSS Cyclops*, a steamer bound

for Malaya. For the return journey, and as the Second World War was declared, he changed ships – to the *TSS Menelaus* - and eventually gravitated to a career in the Royal Air Force. First as an air-gunner, then as a pilot, and subsequently as a flight-instructor. Horsley was later attached to the Communications-Squadron of the 2nd Tactical Air Force in France. And, during the D-Day invasion of Normandy, he accepted the job of personal pilot to Major-General Sir Miles Graham. He returned to England in 1947, joined the staff of the Central Flying School, 23 Training Group, and was appointed Adjutant to the Oxford University Air Squadron in 1948.

In July 1949, Horsley entered the Royal Household as a Squadron Leader, and as Equerry to Her Royal Highness, the Princess Elizabeth, Duchess of Edinburgh (better known today as Her Majesty, Queen Elizabeth II), and to His Royal Highness, the Duke of Edinburgh. In 1952, Horsley became a Wing-Commander and in 1953 became a full-time Equerry to the Duke of Edinburgh; it was a role he held until 1956.

From the latter part of the 1950s to the early 1960s, Horsley was employed as Senior-Instructor at the RAF Flying College, Manby, Lincolnshire; as Commanding-Officer at RAF Wattisham, Suffolk; and as Group-Captain, Near-East Air Force (NEAF), Operations, on the island of Cyprus. Horsley made the rank of Air Vice-Marshal; later attaining the position of Assistant-Chief of Air-Staff

(Operations), and then that of Commanding-Officer, 1-Group from 1971 to 1973. His final post in the Royal Air Force was as the Deputy-Commander-in-Chief of Strike Command, which he held from 1973 to 1975.

And there's one more thing: Horsley's other claim to fame is that, in late 1954, he had a face-to-face encounter with a human-looking alien who went by the memorable and mysterious name of Mr. Janus.

"What is your interest in flying saucers?"

The very strange affair began when Horsley learned of the Duke of Edinburgh's fascination with the complexities of the UFO puzzle. According to Horsley: "[The Duke] was quite interested. As always his mind was open. He agreed I should do a study on the subject in my spare time; as long as I kept it in perspective and didn't bring the Palace into disrepute. He didn't want to see headlines about him believing in little green men."

With typical British understatement, Horsley said: "At the end of my tour at the Palace, I had a very strange experience."

To say the least!

Sir Arthur Barratt, who worked at Buckingham Palace, as Gentleman Usher to the Sword of State, introduced Horsley to a certain General Martin, who, in turn, put him in touch with a mysterious Mrs. Markham. Interestingly, the English researchers Dr. David Clarke and Andy Roberts learned from Horsley that General Martin "believed UFOs were visitors from an alien civilization which wanted to warn us of the dangers posed by atomic war." According to Horsley, it was Mrs. Markham who told him – in an *earlier* meeting, which will be described shortly - to turn up at a particular apartment in London's Chelsea district on a specific evening, where he would meet a stranger: the aforementioned Mr. Janus.

Allegedly, the apartment – on Smith Street - was the home of Mrs. Markham; although, as we'll see, there are solid reasons to believe Mrs. Markham had far stranger origins and dwellings than London, England. Nevertheless, she reportedly sat in on the conversation between Horsley and Mr. Janus – albeit without uttering even a single, solitary word.

Horsley said of his chat with the man that: "Janus was there, sitting by the fire in a deep chair. He asked: 'What is your interest in flying saucers?' We talked for hours about traveling in space and time. I don't know what or who he was. He didn't say he was a visitor from another planet but I had that impression. I believe he was here to observe us. I never saw him again. I have no qualms about the reaction to my experience with Mr. Janus."

Rather disturbingly, and echoing the claims of so many of the Contactees that the Space-Brothers were concerned by our ever-growing nuclear arsenals, UFO investigator

Timothy Good says: "In my second and last meeting with Sir Peter Horsley at his home in 2000, he revealed that, in addition to being disturbed by the realization that Janus was reading his mind, he was even more disturbed by the fact that this extraordinary man 'knew all Britain's top-secret nuclear secrets.'"

In light of what Mr. Janus knew, is it possible that this bizarre episode was actually part of some state-sponsored operation designed to ascertain the nature of Sir Peter's character and his loyalty to the country? This particularly novel and thought-provoking theory was most assuredly on the minds of researchers Clarke and Roberts, who asked Horsley if he considered it feasible that he had been "set up" by MI5 to "test his vulnerability."

Horsley provided the pair with an adamant, "no."

Right up until his death in 2001, Horsley's position on the overwhelmingly weird experience was rock-solid: "I don't care what people think - it was what happened. I would say they come from another planet somewhere in the universe but not in our galaxy. They are benign, not aggressive and, like us, are explorers."

The investigation begins

All of this brings us back to Brian Kinnersley, who says that, in 1955, an MI5 investigation of Sir Peter Horsley's claims began. It was a small-scale operation comprised of just Kinnersley's grandfather and three other individuals. It lasted for, at most, two or three weeks. According to Kinnersley, various scenarios were looked at, such as the possibility that this was some sort of alternative and ingenious Soviet ruse to try and uncover British defense secrets of an atomic nature. The idea that it may have been an American, rather than a Russian, operation was also addressed. Despite intensive digging, nothing solid – or even vague – surfaced that might have suggested Mr. Janus was not an alien, but a player with one of the super-powers instead, who was using a UFO-themed cover to try and secure British state-secrets. This led MI5 to then consider the most incredible scenario possible: that Mr. Janus was, indeed, an extraterrestrial visitor after all, one who was deeply concerned by the possibility that the human race was on the verge of exterminating itself.

Brian Kinnersley's grandfather had extensive meetings with Sir Peter, during which the latter related something very intriguing. It focused on the aforementioned "Mrs. Markham," described by Horsley himself as "enigmatic" and who was responsible for arranging the historic meeting between Horsley and Janus. Horsley apparently had a very good reason for describing the mysterious woman as an enigma. According to MI5's records, Horsley stated that he had his deep suspicions Mrs. Markham was a human-looking alien, too. Based on what is about to be revealed, you may very well agree.

Late one February 1955 evening, in the confines of a

plush, elite club near Whitehall, London, Horsley described – to Kinnersley's grandfather – the process by which he came to encounter Mrs. Markham. It went like this: Sir Arthur Barratt, a Gentleman Usher to the Sword of State at Buckingham Palace, knew of the Duke of Edinburgh's interest in flying saucers. And, so, when he learned that the duke had urged Horsley to quietly investigate the UFO controversy, Barratt referred Horsley to an American Air Force general whose last name was Martin. Barratt, apparently, had come to know Martin in 1953 and learned that he worked in the U.K., with a NATO contingent, at a military base in Suffolk, England. Horsley stressed there was nothing even remotely alien about General Martin. But that could most definitely not be said about Mrs. Markham – not at all.

MI5 continued to put the pieces of the puzzle together.

Mrs. Markham enters the scene

Brian Kinnersley was told by his grandfather that General Martin claimed to know something astonishing and not a little disturbing. In fact, it was *highly* disturbing. The general quietly informed Sir Peter, as they sat in the latter's home and sipped fine brandy, that nothing less than a race of extremely human-looking aliens were among us – and in most of the leading nations on the planet, no less. It was a case of outright alien infiltration, said General Martin, who added that, within the Pentagon, people were in two minds as to whether this was a benevolent infiltration or something that was soon destined to mutate into something very dark. It was clear to Martin's sources that the aliens were particularly concerned by our atomic arsenals. But, whether that concern was for us, or for the planet itself - which some Pentagon high-ups suspected the ETs might want to claim as their own - was a matter of deep and, occasionally, furious debate. All of this brings us to Mrs. Markham.

Sir Peter listened, surely entranced and not a little concerned, as General Martin informed him that via an intermediary, he – Horsley - could actually have a face-to-face encounter with an alien. Which, as we have seen, turned out to be the curiously named Mr. Janus. That intermediary was Mrs. Markham, who Horsley met shortly before the meeting with Janus. The general advised Sir Peter to expect a visit from Mrs. Markham, and that he should be prepared, and should steady himself, for something profound. That was an understatement of epic proportions. According to Horsley, General Martin appeared to greatly fear Mrs. Markham, something which, he said, was provoked by her "not quite looking properly human," as Brian Kinnersley tantalizingly worded it.

Having got the lowdown on the Janus-Horsley debate, MI5 then backtracked and got into the matter of Mrs. Markham.

Unnerving, unsmiling, unblinking

At around 8:00 p.m. – the night before Sir Peter Horsley
had his encounter with Mr. Janus - there was a loud knock
at the door. *She* had arrived. Sir Peter was confronted by
a woman dressed in a long, black, thick coat and wearing
black heels. Her black hair was worn long and straight, and
her skin was like that of someone in an anemic state. Vampire-like might have been a far better description. Or, perhaps, Vampira meets Elvira. Horsley said he felt decidedly
ill at ease in the company of the woman who stood before
him, who introduced herself only as Mrs. Markham, and
who had an unsettling, emotion-free appearance and voice.
"Monotone" was how her words were described. Despite
immediately developing a distinct sense that Mrs. Markham
was not someone to cross paths with, and who was likely not
even human, Sir Peter invited her in. She simply nodded
and strode right past him and proceeded to look around the
rooms of Horsley's abode. The slightly shocked Sir Peter did
nothing but follow her, unsure of what her curious behavior
meant. He was even more shocked when *she* invited *him* to
take a seat!

Horsley told MI5 that just like Mr. Janus, Mrs.
Markham did not explicitly state that she was from another
world – ever - but her words made it clear to him that,
at the *very* least, she was in contact with such beings and
could arrange a meeting with them. Despite the disturbing,

unearthly atmosphere that the presence of Mrs. Markham provoked, Sir Peter kept his calm. The unblinking, unsmiling, pale beauty before him warned that the Earth was in grave danger – the reason being the threat posed by the growing atomic arsenals of NATO and the Soviet Union, of course. He, Horsley was told, could significantly aid in lessening tensions between the super-powers, providing he was willing to come on-board with a group of extraterrestrials that wished to see the Earth completely disarmed of its atomic technology.

Hardly surprisingly, Sir Peter was highly suspicious of all this, fearing that if disarmament occurred, on both sides, it would then leave everyone on Earth vulnerable and wide open to attack from something potentially far worse than the Soviets – and he said so, out loud. Mrs. Markham, in return, offered no reply, beyond that of a slight, wry smile. Her *only* smile, in the entire meeting, which may tell us more than a bit about the woman's motivations. Nevertheless, Horsley said he would be willing to meet with Mrs. Markham's sources - namely, the aliens. And, so it was that four or five days later, Sir Peter Horsley had his now infamous head-to-head with Mr. Janus – thanks to Mrs. Markham, who provided Horsley with the Chelsea, London address at which he could find Mr. Janus on the night in question.

With the conversation over, Mrs. Markham simply nodded, stood up, and exited Horsley's home – vanishing into the English darkness, not unlike some sinister specter in an old, black-and-white, Bela Lugosi movie. Rather intriguingly, according to Horsley, after he retired to bed that same night, he was woken in the early hours by an ear splitting wailing, in the tones of what was clearly a woman. In a cold sweat, Horsley froze – that is until the wailing came to a sudden end after fifteen or twenty seconds. One could make a good case that what Horsley experienced was the cry of a banshee; a wild, black-haired, Irish she-spirit that often delivers messages of looming death and misfortune. Might Mrs. Markham have been just such a thing? In light of her appearance, one suspects that particular theory may well have crossed Sir Peter's mind as he lay there in bed, filled with nothing but stone-cold fear.

Horsley would see Mrs. Markham one more time – as we have seen, when Horsley, Markham, and Janus were altogether, in that darkly-lit London apartment.

As an appropriately odd postscript, Janus was never to be seen again. General Martin became "distant and evasive." And, as for Mrs. Markham, she was nowhere to be seen. When Sir Peter decided to make a follow-up visit to what was said to have been Mrs. Markham's apartment, there was no answer. According to the neighbors, the woman who lived there had "left in a hurry."

An ominous and terrifying harbinger of death: the banshee.
(Thomas Crofton Croker, 1825).

Mars' devil girl comes to life

Brian Kinnersley's grandfather revealed to his colleagues at MI5 precisely what Horsley had told him – about both Mrs. Markham and Mr. Janus. Despite a bit of good-natured ribbing, one of Kinnersley's co-workers on the project observed that Mrs. Markham sounded incredibly like the lead character in a movie that had been released at cinemas in the U.K. in 1954 – the very same year as Horsley's encounters in London. It was a movie the man in question, a fan of sci-fi, had seen when it was released. Its title: *Devil Girl from Mars* – the "Devil Girl" of the title being a woman who does indeed come across astonishingly like Mrs. Markham, as we shall now see.

A black-and-white science-fiction film, *Devil Girl from Mars* starred Patricia Laffan as the Devil Girl of the movie's title, along with Hazel Court, who appeared in a number of classic Hammer Film Productions horror-movies of the late 1950s and 1960s. Basically, the film tells the story of a sultry and sinister alien babe from Mars named Nyah, who spends the whole time clad in, and strutting around in, a tight-fitting black outfit, black cloak and long black-boots. She comes to our world to seek out males to help boost the waning Martian population. As Nyah reveals to those she encounters, Mars has been decimated as a result of a war on the red planet between males and females; a war the women won. With the Martian men now almost gone, this makes breeding more than a significant problem.

The plan is for Nyah to land her flying saucer in the very heart of London and announce to the people of the U.K. – and, soon thereafter, to the entire world – that a program of alien-human breeding is to quickly begin in earnest. Like it or like it not. I can't say it sounds bad at all. Unfortunately for Nyah, things go deeply awry and her spacecraft comes down near an old inn in the dark wildernesses of Scotland. It's an inn that is populated by just the owner, a couple of employees and a handful of guests. And, yes, as you might have quickly guessed, they become the small, heroic band that has to try and thwart Nyah's dastardly plans to enslave the entire human race. Or, at least, the world's men.

Devil Girl From Mars certainly isn't a classic of the genre.

But it is entertaining and thought-provoking. Not only that: it also contains a number of Contactee-based parallels. For example, Nyah comes across not unlike Truman Bethurum's Aura Rhanes. Nyah can speak all Earth-based languages, as, reportedly, could Captain Rhanes. She warns of the perils of war and destruction, as did pretty much all of the aliens that absolutely dominated 1950s-era Ufology. She provides a wealth of obscure scientific data about her craft to those of the group she invites on-board, which is a curious theme present in many Contactee accounts. And she is strangely and noticeably detached and even slightly ethereal – further characteristics of eerie Aura Rhanes.

On top of that there is the matter of Nyah's race visiting the Earth as a means to try and save the waning Martian population. Today, we hear a great deal about alien abductions, and the so-called black-eyed, diminutive Grays, and the theories that they are on an evolutionary decline. The result: they come to the Earth to abduct people. They then reap DNA, sperm and eggs, which they use as part of a bizarre and nightmarish program to create a hybrid species that is part-human and part-E.T.

Back in the 1950s, when *Devil Girl from Mars* was made, however, many people within Ufology were focusing on the idea that extraterrestrials were here to "save" us from the perils of atomic destruction in *The Day the Earth Stood Still*-style. Or, to destroy us in scenarios akin to those presented in *War of the Worlds* and *Invasion of the Body Snatchers*. For the most part, the idea that inter-species cross-breeding was at the very heart of the alleged alien mission didn't surface until years later. So, for that reason alone, it's interesting that *Devil Girl from Mars* is heavily focused around the specific angle of alien-human cross breeds that dominates so much of alien abduction research today.

When the clear parallels between Sir Peter Horsley's encounter with Mrs. Markham and those of Mars' black-clad "devil girl" became clear, Horsley was quite naturally questioned by MI5, to see if he had seen the movie. It was, without doubt, a logical question to ask. The movie, after all, was made in 1954 and Horsley's encounters occurred in that year, too. For his part, Sir Peter flatly denied ever seeing *Devil Girl from Mars*. Nor had he ever heard of it. He did, however – when told of the plotline of the movie - ponder on the theory that, just perhaps, the human-looking aliens in our midst that General Martin told of, had also infiltrated the domain of movie-making – to the extent they were now secretly shaping and manipulating our perceptions of aliens, via on-screen entertainment.

Whatever the truth of this very strange affair and its cast of notable characters – the clandestine agents of MI5, the Duke of Edinburgh, Sir Peter Horsley, General Martin, Sir Arthur Barratt, and that pale-skinned, black-clad vamp that called herself Mrs. Markham – it demonstrates that the WIB have the unnerving ability to get their grips into some of the most senior and influential figures in both government and the military. Including those like Sir Peter himself, a man who had official clearance to launch the nukes that could have ensured the end of human civilization. A disturbing thought, for sure. Equally disturbing, and as we'll later see, in the 1970s another WIB got close to a powerful figure in government. On that occasion, the figure was U.S. President Richard M. Nixon.

4

"It was as if she were dead"

The mid-to-late 1960s was a period when encounters with the Women in Black reached near-fever-pitch levels. It all began in early spring 1967, when reports began to surface of black-garbed "gypsy women" roaming around certain, quieter parts of New York. They clearly weren't regular gypsies, however. That much was made clear by the fact that they exclusively targeted those who had undergone UFO encounters. Odder still, on more than a few occasions, the alleged gypsy women were seen in the dead of night, standing as still as statues and staring malevolently into the homes of people who claimed close encounters with alien entities. Attempts to confront them were met with outright hostility – something that made even the homeowners back away in fear.

One of the weirdest of all the early 1967 cases occurred in the vicinity of Melville, New York, and involved a rancher whose farm was located in a rural, isolated part of town. Only days before he received a most unwelcome visit, the man saw a definitive flying saucer hovering over one of his fields, and which – somewhat amazingly – had what was described as a "ladder" hanging from its underside. At least, until the ladder was hastily retracted and the saucer shot away, high into the sky, and vanished from view. That was hardly the end of the matter, however.

Just a few days later, the man heard a knock at the door. Given that his home was in the middle of pretty much nowhere, he opened the door both slowly and cautiously. Stood before him was a "Gypsy lady" who was dressed in a gray dress that reached her ankles and who wore sandals. Just like so many of the Men in Black, her skin was noted for its deep, olive complexion, and her eyes were described as "Oriental." The rancher added that she stood around five-feet and four inches tall, and had long hair that was "so black" it "looked dyed."

The woman said to the slightly alarmed man: "I have traveled a long way. May I have a glass of water? I must take a pill."

Baffled, the man decided not to risk incurring her wrath and quickly fetched her a glass of water and watched as she swallowed a round, green-colored pill. She thanked him, turned, and walked away – which the man found very strange, given that he lived on a backroad, and walking to the nearest town would be an arduous task, to say the least.

John Keel said of this acutely odd and disconcerting episode: "'I have traveled a long way' is an old Masonic pass phrase and is frequently used in these contacts." He added:

"The pill-taking ploy is also a common procedure. When a most peculiar being visited a family on Cope May, New Jersey, early in 1967, he also took a pill. He too had 'traveled a long way,' and after conducting an inane interview with the family, he stepped into the night, got into a black Cadillac, and drove off with the lights out."

```
"There was almost something mystical about her
appearance and grace"
```

Back in the early summer of 1967 – thanks to an introduction made by a woman named Jaye P. Paro, a host on Babylon, New York's WBAB station – John Keel met with a girl who had a fascinating story to tell. It was a disturbing story too, as *every single one* of those involving the WIB most assuredly are. Given the controversial nature of the affair, Keel agreed to always, and only, refer to her as Jane. Just like the WIB, Jane stood out from the crowd; in her case, however, it was in a positive fashion, as Keel noted: "She was a very sensitive woman, more ethereal than sensual. There was almost something mystical about her appearance and grace."

At the time in question, there was a wealth of very unsettling activity going on in the Mount Misery area of Huntington, New York, a place about which researcher Arthur Criscione says: "Locals have called the area Mount Misery for centuries but you will never find it written that way on any map. It got its name because of its unfarmable land and the steep hills. Since the area was not conducive to growing food, it became a crossroads between farming communities and the difficult trek caused many a wagon wheel to snap."

The foreboding area was, and still is, a veritable magnet for paranormal activity: ghostly, glowing-eyed, and black-haired hounds prowl around the landscape; mysterious, black cars cruise the roads; and spectral children and adults – some of a classic "phantom hitchhiker" variety – wander along the old pathways, always by night. And then there are Mount Misery's UFOs, sightings of which reached their peak in the early months of 1967. Not surprisingly, the local kids immediately caught wind of the reports. And, as a result, on dark, weekend nights, girl- and boy-friends would drive around the area, looking for flying saucers, and, under canopies of trees and darkness, doing what young lovers do on Saturday nights all around the world. This included Jane and her love, Richard.

It was one particularly chilly and dark Saturday evening in mid-May 1967 when Jane and Richard were driving around the roads of Mount Misery and when Richard, quite out of the blue, fell ill. He managed to pull the car to the side of the road, immediately after which he fainted at the wheel. Panic-stricken Jane didn't know what to do. As it transpired, the decision of what to do next was suddenly, and violently, taken out of her by-now-clammy hands. A near-blinding white light flooded the vehicle, having originated somewhere in the deep, almost impenetrable, woods that surrounded the car. Jane found herself completely immobilized in her seat by some unseen, paranormal force. It's clear there was a degree of missing time involved, since the next thing the couple remembered was driving along Mount Misery's Old County Road, some distance from where all of the terror exploded. That was barely the start of the high-strangeness, however.

"I have messages concerning Earth and its people"

A couple of days later Jane experienced something that is a common factor in both WIB and MIB encounters: an odd and somewhat disturbing telephone call. The mysterious woman at the other end of the line did not identify herself to Jane, but – in a weird, "metallic"-sounding style – instructed Jane to go to her local library, to ask the staff for a specific book on Native American history, and to then turn to page forty-two and read it. *Very* carefully. It was an extremely curious request (one which bordered upon an order), but Jane felt oddly drawn to follow the instructions of her anonymous Woman in Black.

Jane reached the library around mid-morning. Even her arrival was dominated by profound oddities: aside from the librarian and Jane herself, the building was completely empty of people and was vacuum-like in its silence and still-ness. As for that same librarian, well...

Jane described her as only a Woman in Black can be described: her hair was black, her eyes were "very black," her skin was olive, and her black-colored outfit was curiously out of time. In Jane's words, the WIB was dressed in "an old-fashioned suit like something out of the 1940s, with a long skirt, broad shoulders, and flat old-looking shoes." Most astonishing of all, before Jane could say anything, the WIB handed her – from under a desk - a copy of the very book Jane had been instructed to seek out by her mysterious caller.

Jane, unsettled, but determined to find out what was going on, took a seat, opened the book and turned to page forty-two. As she did so, the writing on the page changed from large to small, and back again, several times. Rather amazingly, the writing then did something else: it magically morphed into a message. Jane was able to remember the entire, length message – word for word – something that suggested it had been subliminally implanted in her mind. She carefully wrote it down:

"Good morning, friend. You have been selected for many reasons. One is that you are advanced in auto-suggestion. Through this science we will make contact. I have messages concerning Earth and its people. The time is set. Fear not. I am a friend. For reasons best known to ourselves you must make your contacts known to one reliable person. To break this code is to break contact. Proof shall be given. Notes must be kept of the suggestion state. Be in peace."

With that, Jane stood up from the chair and closed the book. The WIB was nowhere to be seen. Jane was all alone in a deserted, silent library. To say she fled the place in terror would be an understatement. Before we return to the story of Jane, it's worth noting an incredibly similar incident to that involving Jane. It occurred one particular day in mid-November 1980 and revolved around an encounter with an MIB – *also* in a near-deserted library.

"Flying saucers are the most important fact of the century"

On the day in question, Peter Rojcewicz was working on his PhD thesis in folklore. It was while doing research at the Library of the University of Pennsylvania that Rojcewicz had an encounter of a type that will instantly be recognizable, in terms of its relation to Jane's, some thirteen years earlier. Rojcewicz's very own words are suggestive of the menace that was soon to follow: "It was a strange day, weather-wise, with erratic shifts of rain and wind and sun. It would get very blustery, and then it would become very calm. It was approximately 4:30 P.M. and already on the dark side."

As Rojcewicz studied hard, and as nightfall loomed, he suddenly became aware of a darkly-clad, tall and thin man in his midst. The odd character had tanned skin, black and greasy hair, sunken eyes, and a hard to define accent, but one that had a strong European flavor to it. In addition, he wore a Texan-style string tie. Its color doesn't even need describing; one and all surely can surely deduce that by now.

The man asked Rojcewicz what he was working on, and Rojcewicz told him that he was researching the UFO phenomenon. The MIB then proceeded to ask Rojcewicz if he had ever seen a UFO. He replied he was more interested in accounts of UFOs than whether or not they were alien craft. The MIB was not happy by Rojcewicz's response. In a loud voice he said, "Flying saucers are the most important fact of the century, and you're not interested?!" The man then stood up – "as if mechanically lifted" – put his hand on Rojcewicz' shoulder, and added, as he walked away, "Go well in your purpose."

Now we come to the part that closely parallels the story of Jane, her Woman in Black, and the empty library. Rojcewicz later said of how the encounter came to its end: "Within, say, ten seconds, great fear overwhelmed me and for the first time I entertained the idea that this man was otherworldly. Really, I was very frightened. I got up, walked two steps in the direction he had left in, turned around, and returned again to my seat. Got up again. *I was highly excited and finally walked around the stacks to the reference desk and nobody was behind the desk. In fact, I could see no one at all in the library. I've gone to graduate school, and I've never been in a library when there wasn't somebody there! No one was even at the information desk across the room.* [Note from the author: italics mine]. I was close to panicking and went quickly back to my desk. I sat down and tried to calm myself. In about an hour I rose to leave the library. There were two librarians behind each of the two desks!"

And, now, back to Anne.

The zombie woman

Like her boyfriend, Richard – after the experience out at Mount Misery - Jane was soon feeling very ill, suffered from vomiting and developed a fever. The sickness eventually went away, but, as it did so, something else began in earnest. Almost everywhere Jane would go, she would see the creepy WIB/librarian. As just two examples of many: on June 5, the Woman in Black turned up at the same gas station where Jane was having her tank filled. Jane could barely manage a fear-filled nod, as an acknowledgment to the woman's menacing, murderous smile. The next day, the WIB appeared in a department store in town and tried to engage Jane in what was an odd, stilted form of English.

From what Jane had to say, the WIB seemed downright zombified: she moved in a jerky, juddering fashion, her eyes stared with malevolence, and her words made little sense. Jane told John Keel that, regarding the WIB, "It was as if she were dead." Most hair-raising of all, when Jane tried to make conversation with the woman, and asked if she lived locally, the WIB replied with nothing but a wailing, crone-like, hysterical laugh.

The woman then asked a most curious question: "Is there any AU here?" Jane had no idea what this meant. The WIB suddenly vanished from sight. John Keel made an intriguing observation on this question: "Just that week I had been pondering the significance of gold in UFO and religious lore. Gold is the seventy-ninth element and the chemical symbol for it is AU."

One has to wonder if the Woman in Black's question was in some way linked to the earlier- discussed issue concerning Albert Bender and the fascination that both the WIB and the MIB have for alchemy – the transformation of base metals into precious ones, including gold, or AU.

"I am Apol"

As if all that was not strange enough, the surreal factor only began to increase for Jane. Early the following morning, Jane decided to take a walk. It was barely dawn, and the town was still shrouded in shadows. As she walked passed a particularly dark alley, the Woman in Black loomed into view, as if from nowhere, or from some nightmarish realm: "Peter is coming. Why are you interested in our mount? Peter is coming very soon," were her odd and icily delivered words. For Jane, the words were a reference to Catholic teachings that the final Pope would be named Peter.

Then, out of the blue, came a black Cadillac, the absolute calling card of the MIB. It came to a screeching halt

next to the two women, and out of one of the rear doors
came an unsettling-looking character. It was a man dressed
in a dark grey suit, with an "oriental" appearance, and who
sported a disturbing, almost maniacal, grin. The driver, said
Jane, seemed almost identical in appearance. The man with
the fearsome grin shook Jane's hand and said, "I am Apol."
Jane said that holding Apol's hand was like holding the
hand of a cold corpse.

The man gave Jane a piece of parchment that contained
a metallic disc, in terms of size around that of a quarter. Jane
- who later said that throughout this entire, odd experience,
she feel light-headed and spaced-out – announced to the
WIB and Apol that she was going to mail both items to
someone, who happened to be Keel, although she did not
tell the pair who, exactly. Evidently, both the WIB and the
MIB were happy, since they again suddenly sported cold,
eerie grins. The black Cadillac immediately returned and
whisked the pair away for destinations unknown, but surely
no good.

According to Keel, when the package arrived it contained nothing unusual: just an old envelope and a nameless
ID tag. Clearly, this was not what Jane had mailed to Keel
just days earlier. So, Keel mailed the items back to Jane. Cue
even more strangeness: when Jane opened the package, she
was overwhelmed by a smell of sulfur – a classic aspect of
paranormal and demonic activity and presence, and something which Albert Bender noted in his experiences with

the Men in Black in the early 1950s. On top of that, the disk was discolored: originally silver it was now a very appropriate black. Keel said of this situation: "The implication was clear. Someone had the ability to intercept the US mails and tamper with things in sealed envelopes!"

The bizarre activity continued: Jane had further, nonsensical run-ins with Apol. She was visited and quizzed by mysterious, military men who turned out not to be military men, after all. And, Jane was given predictions about dire, forthcoming events in the Middle East. Like so many people who have found themselves plunged into the world of the WIB and the MIB, Jane had no answers for what it was that briefly toyed with her, and tormented her, back in 1967.

It's worth noting, too, that John Keel told of a further, mysterious woman in the vicinity of Mount Misery in this very same time frame: "This was a woman with striking white hair who claimed to represent a local newspaper. She carried a book 'like a big ledger' and asked the witness a number of personal questions about her family background. When I later checked with the newspaper I found they employed no one of that description."

Who this additional weird woman was, Keel never found out. And, apparently, neither did anyone else.

Dazed and confused

There is another aspect to all of this that requires addressing and commenting on. At the same time Jane was being targeted by that odd WIB/librarian, Jaye P. Paro, of Babylon, New York's WBAB station, was also encountering others of that same, eerie ilk. On one particular night, around 8:00 p.m., Paro was out walking when the ubiquitous black Cadillac arrived on the scene. Rather oddly, when the driver of the car pulled up alongside her, and a rear window was wound down, Paro got in the back of the vehicle without a second thought. She later said: "There was a funny smell inside. Antiseptic, like a hospital. And there were flashing lights on the dashboard. I couldn't take my eyes off them. I felt like they were hypnotizing me."

On top of that, one of the MIB in the vehicle waved a small bottle under Paro's nose, which seemingly contained something that had the ability to take away her willpower and placed her under the control of the MIB, who proceeded to ask a variety of nonsensical questions – something they are renowned for doing. Paro, dazed and confused, was later returned to the exact same spot from where she was picked up. As will become apparent in the next chapter, Paro's experience was mirrored by a near-identical affair, in which the strange contents of a bottle were used - by a WIB - to render a woman into a slave-like state. More fascinating, the woman in question worked for none other than President Richard M. Nixon.

Before we get to the matter of the only U.S. president to resign from office, it's worth noting that the matter of MIB, a weirdly-lit car, and a person rendered into an altered state of mind, were all staple parts of the famous UFO landing at Rendlesham Forest, England in December 1980.

A glowing car and weirdness in the woods

The man we have to thank for bringing this matter to our attention is Larry Warren. He is one of the key players in the Rendlesham case and (with Peter Robbins) the author of *Left at East Gate*. It's vital reading for anyone interested in what went down in the woods, and on those fateful nights, thirty-five years ago. While there are various opinions and ideas relative to the Rendlesham Forest timeline, all of those who have studied the case – including the witnesses – conclude that there was not just one night of activity, but several. Things began on December 26 and continued on. It's one of these latter encounters we have to now focus our attention on.

Along with a number of his comrades, Warren was ordered to make his way into the woods. The scene was as amazing as it was surreal: When the group arrived at a clearing, they could see that the immediate vicinity was lit up by an eerie mist. Tensions were high. Wild rabbits and deer were seen fleeing the area, as if for their very lives. Dozens of people were swarming around, some with camera equipment, and others with Geiger-counters. Something weird was going down. Something *very* weird. Out of the blue, a small ball of light headed towards the mist, then came to a sudden halt, hanging directly over it. In seconds, and amid a powerful flash, the light was gone. In its place was a not particularly large object that was pyramid-like in shape.

It wasn't long before something incredible happened: a large ball of gold/blue light surfaced from the side of the craft, maneuvered slowly, and came to a halt about three or so meters before the military personnel. Contained within the ball were a trio of small creatures. They were clearly not human. That much was made obvious by their large heads and cat-like eyes. Warren recalls some kind of dialog occurring between the entities and a military officer – following which Warren and his comrades were told to return to the truck in which they had arrived. All of which brings us to the matter of the glowing car.

Early on the following evening, Warren – on base but off-duty at the time – received a phone call. The caller ordered Warren to head down to the dorm parking area, and to be there in twenty minutes. Warren was additionally told to keep a look out for a dark-colored sedan. Puzzled, Warren did exactly as he was told. And, sure enough, there was the car. So, Warren walked over to it. With hindsight, that may not have been a good idea.

Two men in black suits – classic MIB, one might be

justified in saying – directed him to one of the rear doors of the car. Warren followed their orders and got in the vehicle. At that point, things got even weirder. A strange, green glow dominated the interior of the sedan. It wasn't just illuminated: it was *glowing*. On top of that, Warren began to feel strange, as if he had been suddenly drugged. Distinct shades of Jaye P. Paro's experiences, to be sure.

From there, Warren recalls being groggily taken to an underground portion of the base – possibly one that was *extremely* deep – and where he encountered, from one side of a Plexiglas window, what may very well have been something unearthly. In Warren's own words, as presented in *Left at East Gate*: "I stepped into the confined area and felt as if I was no longer on Earth. I found myself looking into a gigantic, dark cavernous space. It reminded me of the interior of the Houston Astrodome in a strange way. Beads of humidity rolled down the other side of the seamless glass."

A shadowy, small figure was vaguely seen behind the glass, and a strange and brief "conversation" occurred. It was one in which Warren visualized words and pictures in his mind. The entity appeared to know much of Warren's life and indicated it came from a realm which he would never be able to understand. Warren later found himself wandering the base, as his mind finally began to return to normal.

For Larry Warren, the experience was over. The memories, however, still remain.

5

"A sinister group of pale-faced women"

In 2015, Dr. David M. Jacobs' book, *Walking Among Us: The Alien Plan to Control Humanity*, was published. As the title alone suggests, this is an extremely controversial book. Although it is heavily focused on so-called "alien abductees," it is not actually about abduction events at all. Rather, its focus is on how abductees are allegedly being used to assist alien-human hybrids whose role it is to infiltrate human society. And, yes, that word "infiltrate" *is* intended to suggest that nothing good can come from all of this. Or, from any of it.

We're talking about the way in which potentially hostile aliens – with no real regard for us, the Human Race – are working towards a certain, fateful day. A day when the Earth will be so heavily infested with these part-ET/part-human *things* that the invasion, take-over, and/or extermination, will be completed before we'll have even a single chance to do anything about it. Yes, I said it was controversial. Even Jacobs notes this when he says: "My research has uncovered a substantial presence of hybrids living on Earth…This book tells how I came to this seemingly ridiculous conclusion."

Indeed, many will find it ridiculous. After all, Jacobs provides details of hybrids seen at a baseball game, yearning for pizza, and visiting Kmart. And that's just the start of things. As Jacobs also states: "I began my journey in the mid-1960s being thrilled that the UFO phenomenon might signal contact with another species. It did, but not in the way that I imagined. The abduction evidence has forced me to evolve into a fearful investigator. I have uncovered the alien reality, as much as I dislike it."

The back-cover of the book gets even more to the point: "Jacobs' human observers have experienced a concealed reality that is literally next door to some of us, and that he believes is about to interact, secretly and insidiously, with the rest of us." This interaction, suggests Jacobs, is leading towards what is referred to throughout the book as "The Change." For us, it's allegedly not going to be a good change. For *them*? Yes.

It must be said that unlike the vast majority of books with an alien abduction component to them, the cases that are cited in *Walking Among Us* cannot be relegated to the worlds of bad dreams, nightmares, and sleep-paralysis – which are often suggested by skeptics as the root-causes of so many abduction stories. The reason being, as I said, that this book is not strictly about abduction events. We're talking about abductees assisting the hybrids in the real world, driving them around, feeding them, teaching them how to dress and blend in, and ultimately preparing them for the day when who knows what might happen.

So, given the extensively detailed, graphic and vivid accounts of the people reportedly brought into the program, the reader has three main choices: to uncritically accept the stories as they are, to outright dismiss them as lies or fantasies, or to read Jacobs' book with an open-mind and see where the stories lead. I suspect, however, this is a book that will very likely polarize people into two camps: the believers and the disbelievers. You will accept that human-looking aliens are among us, that they are growing in numbers, and that they are becoming more and more human-looking as the years go by. Or, put simply, you won't accept it.

Hybrids, WIB and MIB

Now, I have to say that over the years I have read a great deal of far-out material, some of which I find plausible, but much of which I consider to be the wildest, craziest, most paranoid material out there. And I'm totally fine admitting that were it not for one thing in particular, I would firmly place *Walking Among Us* into that second category. It's something which – rather oddly – Jacobs makes no mention of, even though it's staring the reader right in the face. What might that be? The uncanny similarities between the hybrids and Women in Black and the Men in Black.

To say that *Walking Among Us* is filled with WIB- and MIB-like parallels is not an understatement. It's just a matter of recognizing them. Let's take a close and careful look. Jacobs tells us that young hybrids are "sometimes fascinated with writing instruments. Pens and pencils that are common in our world may never be encountered by aliens, who have no need to write."

It so happens the WIB and the Men in Black have a fascination for pens. One case of three I know of will suffice: Mary Hyre was a woman who played an integral role in the series of 1960s-era events that led John Keel to write *The Mothman Prophecies*. In January 1967, Hyre was visited by a creepy, bowl-haired MIB of around 5-feet in height and who had oddly hypnotic eyes. Throughout the encounter, the black-clad "man" kept staring at Hyre's ballpoint pen. To the point where Hyre told him he could keep it. He took it, laughed loud in a strange fashion, and vanished as mysteriously as he first arrived.

Both the WIB and the MIB are noted for their distinct awkwardness around food – both preferring to ingest nothing more than pills. Jacobs' book is packed with accounts of the hybrids reportedly being baffled by food, how it should be eaten (with or without utensils), what should be eaten cooked and what should be eaten raw, and so on. Gareth Medway notes: "A man in a black suit with a pointed chin, 'thyroid eyes' and 'long, tapering fingers' went into Max's Kansas City, New York, and ordered 'food,' being apparently unable to read the menu, and not knowing how to use a knife and fork. He told a waitress he was from 'another world.'"

Mrs. Ralph Butler, of Owatonna, Minnesota, was visited by a mystery-man masquerading as an Air Force officer in May 1967, after a flurry of UFO activity in the area. She offered him a bowl of Jello, which he tried to drink as if it were a liquid!

"I had to show him how to eat it with a spoon," said Mrs. Butler.

In *Walking Among Us*, some of the ET-hybrids are described as looking "sickly," and as having extremely smooth, and very pale, skin. Just like the Women in Black. Jacobs talks about a hybrid being "greatly overdressed for the summer and his slicked-down hairstyle was wrong." That, too, is reminiscent of so many WIB and MIB reports. Both often arrive at the homes of witnesses in vintage, black cars. Jacobs describes how the hybrids are specifically taught to drive. The hybrids are often described as wearing wigs, and particularly so female hybrids who wear their fake hair black and long – as well shall learn in the next two chapters of this book. Why do I mention all this? Because way back in 1967, John Keel found himself plunged into a strange and surreal situation involving alien-human hybrids and Women in Black.

A story that took decades to surface

It's a saga that John Keel extensively investigated but chose never to publish in his lifetime, in any of his books. Why, exactly, remains a mystery. Back in 1967 Keel wrote an article titled "The Strange Case of the Pregnant Woman." It remained unseen, in print, for decades. In fact, until 2014, when it was finally published. The story is focused on a woman named Helen who lived on Long Island, New York, and who had a series of bizarre encounters with alleged extraterrestrial entities, and with mysterious women. The story is also focused on the matter of the birth of Helen's baby, on October 28, 1967. This was no normal pregnancy, however, as we shall see. Helen's story begins on September 26, 1967. But, it appears that things actually kicked off forty-eight hours earlier.

According to Keel, on the morning of the 26th a woman named Pat headed out to a Lutheran church – situated in a small town located on Long Island. Her morning of prayer, however, was interrupted by the presence of an odd, young woman who, said Keel, appeared to be "East Indian," who had olive-colored skin and "dark Oriental eyes" and who was dressed in a dark, gray, sari-like outfit. The Woman in Gray proceeded to tell Pat some deeply personal things about her – Pat's – life. They were things which no one could have possibly known; least of all a total stranger. So disturbed was Pat by the whispery, eerie messages, she fled the church.

Two days later, the aforementioned Helen had a visit at her Long Island home from a woman who sounded uncannily like the woman that confronted Pat during her prayer session, two days earlier. It was mid-afternoon when a deep, resonating, humming sound filled Helen's home. She raced to the window and was amazed to see a "gleaming" craft of flying saucer-style proportions hanging low in the sky. Her amazement was interrupted by her doorbell ringing.

Helen forced herself to move from the window and headed for the door. On opening it she found herself face to face with, as Keel worded it, "an Indian-like lady about 5'9" tall, wearing a gray sari." Her face was "dark and Oriental-like" and she spoke in a very quiet voice. The Woman in Gray asked for a glass of water – so that she could take a pill, she claimed. Helen, puzzled, did as the WIG asked. The odd woman then swallowed the pill, thanked Helen, turned and walked away, and vanished behind a series of thick, tall bushes. In mere seconds, the UFO – still hanging in the sky – shot away at high speed. That was far from being the end of the matter, however.

Four days later, on the late afternoon of the 30th, the WIG was back. Quite out of the blue, she brought up with Helen the matter of alien contact. Given that Helen was six-months pregnant, had a ten-month-old baby, was estranged from her husband and lived alone, she found the whole thing disturbing and even somewhat threatening. What if the woman tried to force her way into the home? After all, in her heavily pregnant state Helen was hardly in a position to do anything about it. Fortunately, no harm came to Helen; the Woman in Gray vanished into the night, after sharing further, odd information of an alien presence on the Earth.

Hours later, things became decidedly chilly: the WIG – who now identified herself as "Chloe" – phoned out of the blue and told Helen to lock all the doors and windows. As in, *right now*. No sooner had Helen done so, when a large, black car pulled up outside, and two black-garbed men exited the vehicle and proceeded to photograph Helen's home – with a camera that had a *red* flash. Panic-stricken, Helen peered through the curtains, and watched as the two men paced back and forth getting different angles of the house. She then raced to the phone and called John Keel – who did his very best to calm Helen. It was only when, a few minutes later, the MIB left that Helen's anxiety finally started to evaporate.

A deeply concerned Keel told Helen to not open the door to any strangers – at all. She didn't need telling! Keel added that he would drive over to see her on the morning of October 3, which he did. However, just before leaving his home, Keel received a call from a mysterious woman who advised him, in no uncertain terms, that it would not be wise for him to make the trip. Keel, well acquainted with such threats from the WIB and the MIB, ignored this attempt at intimidation. Then came the most amazing thing of all:

"Chloe" – Helen told Keel – had called again, stating that "the baby she was expecting belonged to them."

Babies of the alien kind

According to Keel, Helen's baby was born on October 28 – prematurely. It was "dark skinned and had Oriental features." Ring a bell? It should. Keel also noted that three other women gave birth to practically identical babies on the same night. What makes the story even stranger is that Keel learned all four women did not give birth in hospitals, but in what Keel called an "isolated house." The births were traumatic in the extreme: two of the babies later died and one of the women suffered from severe hemorrhaging at the time of giving birth. Although the women were allowed to take the babies home, attempts were later made - *by a sinister group of pale-faced women* - to access the homes of the mothers and kidnap their babies – which, as Keel notes, were clearly of a definitive hybrid nature. Fortunately, on all occasions the attempted abductions were foiled. Keel kept in touch with Helen for a long time, after which she vanished, along with her children. Whether due to abduction or a desire to start a new life somewhere else, remains unknown. For the sake of Helen and her family, we should all hope and pray it was the latter.

A skeptic might say that Keel was simply the victim of a bizarre and elaborately weaved hoax. On the other hand, what Keel was talking about was something that, for the most part, would not surface in Ufology until the 1980s, two decades later. That's when tales of hybrid babies, stolen babies, curious miscarriages, and alien/human offspring became practically commonplace.

On a similar path, in 1977 Keel wrote an article for the now-defunct publication, *Saga UFO Report*. It was titled "Problems of Identity: The Aliens Among Us." Keel noted in his article that he had on file reports of women who fell pregnant after curious UFO encounters. He added: "I have kept in close contact with several of these women and followed the developments with great interest. The children they produced seem exceptionally bright, and are frequently surrounded by poltergeist manifestations."

Keel also noted in his "Problems of Identity" article: "In *Oahspe*, the amazing book written by a New York dentist while in a trance back in the 1880s, there are pages depicting special children with sober faces and deep black eyes who were supposedly hybrids planted here by some unknown force."

Regardless of what one might think about the *Oahspe* controversy, it sounds very much like Keel had been keeping note of what, today, have become infamously known as the Black-Eyed Children. It's notable that in my 2015 book, *Men in Black: Personal Stories and Eerie Adventures*, author and BEC investigator David Weatherly said the following of these junior fiends in black:

"On the surface, there may seem to be few connections between the UFO connected MIB and creepy little kids with black eyes showing up on doorsteps. But, when we delve into the actual accounts, we find numerous similarities. Consider the appearance of both beings.

"The BEKs are usually described as having pale or pasty skin. Some witnesses report that the skin looks 'artificial.' Still other accounts claim that the children have olive toned skin that implies they are of Mediterranean origin. Both of these descriptions are heard in classic MIB encounters. Oddly, no one who has ever encountered the BEKs report a blemish of any kind. Bear in mind, these are children usually in their pre-teen years. One would expect acne, pimples, freckles, something, but it's never the case.

"Next is the manner of speech. The black eyed children are reported to speak in a very monotone manner. Their use of language is often awkward and unusual. They will use phrases that simply aren't natural such as 'Is it food time?' Perhaps even more troubling, many people who encounter the BEKs believe that the children are attempting to exert some type of mind control through the use of repeated phrases and their cold, monotone speech patterns. Typical MIB encounters certainly contain elements of attempted coercion by the strange gentlemen as witnesses to UFO sightings are encouraged to ignore what they saw. Are the attempts by the children another form of this same control dynamic?"

I could go on and on with Keel's early reports of alien-human hybrids, mysterious women, odd-looking kids, and weird pregnancies. Collectively, they demonstrate that Keel really was someone far ahead of his time. He was onto all this way back in 1967. It wasn't until the 1980s and the 1990s (and the 2000s, in terms of the Black-Eyed Children) that most of the rest of Ufology finally caught up.

And we're still not done with 1960s-era Women in Black.

6

"She was black. Her skin was black, her body was black, the wings were black; everything was black"

One of the strangest, and undoubtedly, creepiest of all encounters with a Woman in Black occurred at the height of the Vietnam War, and specifically in Da Nang, a city on the south-central coast of Vietnam. It was in August 1969 that a man named Earl Morrison, along with several comrades, had the shock of his life. It was, very appropriately, in the dead of night when the menacing event occurred – and as the men were on guard-duty, keeping a careful look out for the Vietcong. Everything was quiet and normal until around 1:30 a.m. That's when the atmosphere changed, and an eerie form made its presence known to the shocked men of the U.S. 1st Division Marine Corps. Despite being somewhat reluctant to speak out publicly, Morrison eventually changed his mind and, by 1972, was comfortable about discussing the incident, even if he wasn't comfortable with what he encountered. His story makes for incredible reading:

"We saw what looked like wings, like a bat's, only it was gigantic compared to what a regular bat would be. After it got close enough so we could see what it was, it looked like a woman. A naked woman. She was black. Her skin was black, her body was black, the wings were back; *everything* was black. But it glowed. It glowed in the night, kind of [a] greenish cast to it. She started going over us, and we still didn't hear anything. She was right above us, and when she got over the top of our heads she was maybe six or seven feet up.

"We watched her go straight over the top of us, and she still didn't make any noise flapping her wings. She blotted out the moon once – that's how close she was to us. And dark – looked like pitch black then, but we could still define her because she just glowed. Real bright, like. And she started going past us straight towards our encampment. As we watched her – she had got about ten feet or so away from us – we started hearing her wings flap. And it sounded, you know, like regular wings flapping. And she just started flying off and we watched her for quite a while."

"She resembled the Irish banshee, moaning and
wailing to foretell death in a family"

One of those who took a great deal of interest in the story of the flying woman of Da Nang was a UFO researcher named Don Worley. His personal interview with Morrison revealed additional data, such as the fact that the woman's hair was black and straight, that the wings may have had a slight furry quality to them, that she "rippled" as she flew by, that she appeared to lack bones in her body, and that her wings seemed to be directly "molded" to her hands and arms.

The investigators Janet and Colin Bord say of this particularly odd case: "Usually our reports of winged figures describe them as 'men,' but without any indication whether features are seen which tell the witness definitely that it is a man. In view of this we suspect that so-called 'birdmen' should strictly be termed 'bird people' or 'bird persons,' and that no sex attribution can honestly be made. However, the Da Nang sighting does not come into that category. The only other winged figure we have on record is a creature from Welsh folklore, the Gwrach-y-rhibyn. She resembled the Irish banshee, moaning and wailing to foretell death in a family."

Don't forget that Sir Peter Horsley was shocked from his sleep by a wailing, screaming thing after meeting mysterious Mrs. Markham.

Let' take a closer look at the Gwracg-y-rhibyn.

"Her trailing robes were black"

Marie Trevelyan – a noted expert on Welsh folklore – made more than a few comments that, with the benefit of hindsight, suggests Earl Morrison and his colleagues were visited by something eerily similar to the Gwrach-y-rhibyn. Trevelyan said of the Welsh winged she-monster that it had…

"…long black hair, black eyes, and a swarthy countenance. Sometimes one of her eyes is grey and the other black. Both are deeply sunken and piercing. Her back was crooked, her figure was very thin and spare, and her pigeon-breasted bust was concealed by a somber scarf. Her trailing robes were black. She was sometimes seen with long flapping wings that fell heavily at her sides, and occasionally she went flying low down along watercourses, or around hoary mansions. Frequently the flapping of her leathern bat-like wings could be heard against the window-panes."

Did the Gwrach-y-rhibyn pay a visit to Vietnam in 1969? It's an amazing question to ponder upon. After all, the Welsh monster was noted for her links to looming death. And, no one can deny the tragic number of deaths that occurred during the Vietnam War.

"In its female character it has a trick of crying at intervals, in a most doleful tone"

The exploits and nature of this nightmarish Welsh thing were expertly chronicled back in the 19th century, by a man named Wirt Sykes. At the time, he was the American Consul for Wales. While the story of the Gwrach y Rhibyn is told in Sykes's 1880 book, *British Goblins*, it is to Sykes' original notes we turn our attentions to. They tell a story that is creepy, horrific, and unforgettable:

"A frightful figure among Welsh apparitions is the Gwrach y Rhibyn, whose crowning distinction is its prodigious ugliness. The feminine pronoun is generally used in speaking of this goblin, which unlike the majority of its kind, is supposed to be a female. A Welsh saying, regarding one of her sex who is the reverse of lovely, is, 'Y mae mor salw a Gwrach y Rhibyn,' (She is as ugly as the Gwrach y Rhibyn.)

"The specter is a hideous being with disheveled hair, long black teeth, long, lank, withered arms, leathern wings, and a cadaverous appearance. In the stillness of night it comes and flaps its wings against the window, uttering at the same time a blood-curdling howl, and calling by name on the person who is to die, in a lengthened dying tone, as thus: 'Da-a-a-vy!' 'De-i-i-o-o-o ba-a-a-ch!' The effect of its shriek or howl is indescribably terrific, and its sight blasting to the eyes of the beholder. It is always an omen of death, though its warning cry is heard under varying circumstances; sometimes it appears in the mist on the mountain side, or at cross-roads, or by a piece of water which it splashes with its hands.

"The gender of apparitions is no doubt as a rule the neuter, but the Gwrach y Rhibyn defies all rules by being a female which at times sees fit to be a male. In its female character it has a trick of crying at intervals, in a most

doleful tone, 'Oh! oh! fy ngwr, fy ngwr!' (my husband! my
husband!) But when it chooses to be a male, this cry is
changed to 'Fy ngwraig! fy ngwraig!' (my wife! my wife!) or
'Fy mlentyn, fy mlentyn bach!' (my child, my little child!)
There is a frightful story of a dissipated peasant who met
this goblin on the road one night, and thought it was a living
woman; he therefore made wicked and improper overtures
to it, with the result of having his soul nearly frightened out
of his body in the horror of discovering his mistake. As he
emphatically exclaimed, 'Och, Dduw! it was the Gwrach y
Rhibyn, and not a woman at all.'"

7

"Whatever that young woman did to me, it was like being in a sleepwalk"

It's important to note that the strange saga of Jane, Jaye P. Paro, the empty library, and the "hybrid baby" saga of Helen were not the only examples of a WIB presence in late 1960s-era USA. John Keel found himself reluctantly dragged into the mysterious mix in a very weird fashion. Of the turbulent times from 1966 to 1967 - when his research in and around both West Virginia and Ohio, in relation to the Mothman mystery, was at its height in the town of Point Pleasant - Keel had some very interesting things to say:

"A blond woman in her thirties, well-groomed, with a soft southern accent, visited people in Ohio and West Virginia whom I had interviewed. She introduced herself as 'John Keel's secretary,' thus winning instant admission. The clipboard she carried held a complicated form filled with personal questions about the witnesses' health, income, the type of cars they owned, their general family background, and some fairly sophisticated questions about their UFO sightings. Not the type of questions a run-of-the-mill UFO buff would ask. I have no secretary. I didn't learn about this woman until months later when one of my friends in Ohio wrote to me and happened to mention, 'As I told your secretary when she was here ...' Then I checked and found out she had visited many people, most of whom I had never mentioned in print. How had she located them?"

How, indeed? There was no answer to that question. It's worth noting, however, that Keel uncovered additional cases where clipboard-carrying WIB turned up at people's homes in Point Pleasant, all asking the same kinds of questions that Keel's "secretary" asked, but this time posing as census takers. They were nothing of the sort. But, you knew that, right?

"Earth people do not understand"

Moving onto 1968, there is the story of UFO researcher "Dan O.," which was provided to paranormal authority, Brad Steiger. It was the night of July 13, 1968 when Dan had the great misfortune to cross paths with a Woman in Black. He was on the phone, speaking with a colleague in the UFO field, when their phone call was suddenly, and mysteriously, interrupted. Dan told Steiger: "The third party identified herself as a Mrs. Slago, who, as she said, was accidentally connected with our line. She had been listening to our conversation strictly out of curiosity."

Despite the fact that Mrs. Slago was a complete stranger

and had, according to her, intruded upon the conversation by mistake, Dan decided to tell her about his UFO research, since she had at least heard snippets of what he and his friend had been talking about. As the conversation between Dan and Mrs. Slago progressed, however, the likelihood that her intrusion was all a big mistake, and nothing else, quickly evaporated. Dan's words make that extremely clear. He told Steiger that Mrs. Slago suggested investigating UFOs was not a wise thing to do, and that the matter of UFOs possibly being of alien origin was a matter Dan should steer well clear of.

Dan continued: "She also stated that UFO organizations should not attempt to further the investigation and study of UFOs, because as she put it, 'Earth people do not understand.' She suddenly stopped short of what she was about to say, as if she caught herself about to say something that I should not hear."

Things then got even odder, and somewhat troubling: the woman warned Dan that he should cease his UFO investigations, that it was not wise to speak on the phone about such matters, and that her name was not Slago, after all. It was Nelson, and she worked as a "researcher" for the local police. At that point, Mrs. Slago – or Nelson – abruptly left the conversation. The story wasn't over, however, as Dan demonstrated to Steiger:

"When we checked with the police headquarters, the officers told us that they had no knowledge of either a 'Mrs.

Nelson' or a 'Mrs. Slago' being connected with any phase of police research. Following this incident, we had a complete check made on our telephone lines, but the check revealed no evidence of wire-tapping or anything of that sort. A check with the telephone company revealed that a misconnection of this type could not possibly have been made."

A WIB and the White House

Moving on to the early 1970s, there is a bizarre story that closely parallels – to an uncanny degree - the story of radio-host Jaye P. Paro being drugged by a diabolical band of MIB back in 1967. In a very strange way, this new case involved none other than President Richard M. Nixon and a Woman in Black! The story surfaced on October 23, 1971. The media reported:

"A part-time housekeeper at President Nixon's Key Biscayne retreat has testified she was put in a hypnotic daze by a stranger who told her to shoplift four dresses. Shirley Cromartie, 32, and a mother of three, pleaded no contest Thursday and was given a suspended sentence after law enforcement officers and a psychiatrist testified they believed she was telling the truth. Mrs. Cromartie holds a security clearance to work in the Florida White House, according to testimony. She said a woman met her in a parking lot and asked the time, then ordered her to take the items and bring them to her.

"Mrs. Cromartie testified she fell into a daze when the young woman released a jasmine-like scent from her left hand. 'I just sort of lost my will ... it was a terrifying experience,' she testified. Mrs. Cromartie joined the Key Biscayne White House housekeeping staff about a year ago, according to FBI Agent Leo Mc Clairen. He testified her background was impeccable.

"Dr. Albert Jaslow, a psychiatrist, said he examined her and found she could be hypnotized 'quickly and easily' and believed she was telling the truth. 'But it wasn't the same when he hypnotized me,' Mrs. Cromartie said. 'I couldn't remember anything afterwards. Whatever that young woman did to me, it was like being in a sleepwalk, only awake.'"

As the media continued to dig into the story, things got even stranger. The mysterious woman, with the mind-altering, "jasmine-like scent," was described as being attractive, young, dressed completely in black, and wearing a wig – the latter being something which is a staple part of certain WIB cases, as will become apparent in later chapters. Also, both the WIB and the MIB are oddly fond of asking people the time, as Cromartie's mysterious woman was so very careful to do.

Metro Court Judge, Frederick Barad, said of this surreal saga: "This is all so bizarre that I'm frightened what could happen to the president."

This latter point was something clearly on the mind of

John Keel, too. He speculated that the hypnotic abilities of Cromartie's wig-wearing WIB amounted to "...not some small demonstration for the benefit of President Nixon."

Did the Women in Black target President Richard M. Nixon?
(U.S. Government, 1974).

The breath of the Devil

Almost certainly, "the jasmine-like scent" was a substance that is known officially as scopolamine, but which has a far more ominous slang name: "The Devil's Breath." It is synthesized from the Borrachero Tree, which grows widely in Colombia. Aside from its jasmine-like odor, scopolamine is a powerful drug, exposure to which can almost instantaneously take away a person's free-will, self-preservation, and self-control. To demonstrate its power, there are accounts

– from Colombia - of people exposed to scopolamine emp-
tying their bank-accounts, and handing over their precious
savings to criminals using the drug against unwitting souls.
It's no wonder, then, that Mrs. Cromartie acted in such a
strange, detached, and atypical fashion. But that's not all.

The CIA made great use of scopolamine at the height
of the Cold War, using it on captured Soviet spies and
defecting agents. Britain's intelligence agency, MI6, has even
been rumored to have used scopolamine to provoke trouble-
some characters - those having a bearing on national security issues - into committing suicide. That Mrs. Cromartie
worked for the U.S. Government – and for no less a source
than the President of the United States – makes one wonder if there was some sort of presently unclear connection
between her experience, the Nixon administration, and the
secret CIA world of scopolamine use and manipulation of
the human mind.

There is another side to this story. Many people who
have encountered the WIB have stated that although these
entities are generally highly attractive, there is something
about them – something intangible, hard to define, yet
downright sinister – that makes people want to avoid them,
and at just about all costs possible. As we have seen, however, there are cases where men, despite having alarm bells
ringing in their heads telling them to run like hell, became
entranced and obsessed by the WIB they crossed paths
with. The case of Truman Bethurum and Aura Rhanes is a

perfect example. It transpires that ancient folklore tells of how jasmine has aphrodisiac properties and can be used to not only increase libido, but also to entice a man to become overwhelmingly attracted to one particular woman, almost in slave-like fashion.

Was Shirley Cromartie's WIB an agent of the CIA, using her skills in some strange program that, as John Keel said, was intended as "not some small demonstration for the benefit of President Nixon?" On the other hand, perhaps she was nothing stranger than an opportunist criminal, dosing Cromartie with scopolamine as a means to use her to commit an act of shoplifting. It's worth noting, however, that just like so many other black-garbed WIB she (A) wore a wig, (B) asked Cromartie the time (something the MIB regularly do), and (C) attracted the attention of Keel, leaves wide open the possibility that the woman was far worse than anything that could come out of the criminal underworld of Colombia or the confines of the CIA. A true WIB, she just may have been.

On this latter point, there is yet *another* issue that links President Nixon and the Women in Black. In 1971, the very same year that Shirley Cromartie – an employee of the Nixon administration, as we have seen – ended up in hot water with the police, as a result of her WIB encounter, Nixon himself had a meeting, in the White House's Oval Office, with a famous psychic named Jeane Dixon. President Nixon, via his personal secretary, Rose Mary Woods, was kept abreast of Dixon's claimed psychic predictions, which reportedly included the November 22, 1963 assassination of President John F. Kennedy, and a terrorist attack on the Munich, Germany Olympics in September 1972.

It so transpires that Dixon (who provided astrological readings for Nancy Reagan, when her husband, Ronald Reagan, was president) asserted that her psychic skills were bestowed upon her by none other than "a wandering Gypsy lady." She was very much like the presumed gypsy who, as we have seen, turned up at an isolated farmhouse near Melville, New York, in early 1967, and who scared the living daylights out of the man who made the unfortunate and rash decision to open his front door to her.

That Dixon developed her powers after meeting a female "gypsy," that both Nixon and Reagan had close links to Dixon, and that one of Nixon's staff had an encounter with a very chilling Woman in Black, suggests something ominous: a potential plan on the part of the WIB to try and infiltrate none other than the Oval Office itself.

8

"Her skin was very pale, and of an unusually smooth texture"

In the summer of 2015, I lectured on the mystery of the Men in Black at the monthly meeting of the Phoenix, Arizona, Mutual UFO Network (MUFON) group. After the lecture was over, a group of us headed over to a nearby restaurant. Over dinner, one of the attendees shared with me the details of her very own Woman in Black experience, which occurred in the early 1970s. She was generous enough to later share her story with me – by email – and which reads as follows. It's quite possibly the only Woman in Black case in my files which has a positive outcome attached to it.

"I spent this morning google mapping the route I was on when it happened. In 1972 while driving to Radiology School in the rain about 7:15am on towards I-10 Hi-Rise Bridge, NOLA. Not sure what time of year it was, probably around September. The Bridge: NOLA Industrial Canal Gentilly I 10 Bridge (I-10 High Rise Bridge)."

"I was taken aback by her plain, out of date, odd appearance"

"I was nearing the base of the bridge when I hit slick of water and my car went into a spin. My car turned off. I looked ahead and there was a Mac Truck headed for me and he was on the brakes. I could tell by the water splattering from the sides of the truck. Time stopped and I turned the key. My car started and I drove out of the way. I saw all of the shiny details of the truck's grill and hearing GET in my brain.

"Still brings up an emotion that I can't describe. Like my brain is perceiving 'day to day' time, while at that moment in time, my perception of time changed to actually freezing moments, as if time were obliterated.

"In a slip of time, I pulled off to the side of the road with my life and no collusion. Parked on the shoulder of I-10, I was stunned with my head resting on my steering wheel. Then I heard a knock on my car window. I see this young lady with a gentle looking face, but I was taken aback by her plain, out of date, odd appearance. She was dressed in a black vest and skirt, white blouse, no hat, and a short wave haircut, like my grandmother from the 20's!

"I rolled the window slightly and she talked to me. I felt relieved that someone saw (whatever happened) and cared enough to see if I was okay. Something about her had a stabilizing effect on me. I drove straight to school at Charity

Hospital. It did dawn on me and I kept wondering, why is she dressing like that!??? Even more than why am I still living!??? I was so thanking God for sparing me! I remember Nick, you saying something like this in your lecture: The MIB seem to know before the fact that something will happen, and appear in conjunction with the occurrence, thus you ponder on, as a possible time-travel event. Perhaps, that MIB are keeping the future in line with certain outcomes.

"Good talking today. I do feel that you touched upon something when you link the MIB to time. According to this we are in a state of entropy that would result in disorder. Suppose the MIB are tweaking time to delay or prevent entropy? I have my own proof that time was somehow on my side. Maybe I pulled in another dimension to choose a different outcome? Maybe something chose for me? Thanks for taking this one on."

Moving on...

"She did not speak"

Karen Totten is an artist and sculptor who has had a wealth of anomalous experiences throughout her life, one of which was with an entity that falls definitively into the Woman in Black category

She says: "...when I was 17 I was working in a small convenience store, when a 'woman' came in to buy cigarettes. At first I didn't pay any attention to her until I saw her hand (when she handed me the money) - it was not like a normal human hand. This startled me so I looked up and saw a very pale entity, wearing a thin black coat (like a rain coat) with collar turned up to cover her neck, a heavy long-haired wig, and very large black glasses. This did not entirely hide her strange face: a very pointed chin, scant lip and nose. She did not speak. Took her cigarettes and left! I was kinda stunned. Oddly I cannot remember the details of her hand (though it was the first thing I noticed). Nor do I think she left in a car which was odd since most patrons drove up the store (it was somewhat isolated)."

Karen Totten, witness to a creepy, disguised woman in the 1970s (Karen Totten, 2016).

Totten continues: "…whether this entity is a 'gray' or a 'hybrid', I can only guess. I have never seen what is described as a classic gray alien. Perhaps 'hybrid' is most fitting simply because there seems to be some variety of attributes associated with this general category; i.e. that do not fit perfectly with the classic gray alien type (size of head being foremost). Some details that I do recall with some clarity: First, her skin: it was very pale, white with an almost bluish-gray tint to it, and of an unusually smooth texture. I have never seen anything like it before or since. I had previously seen an albino person; it was nothing like that; i.e., her skin was not UN-pigmented though there was an almost translucent quality to it."

And there were other anomalies, too, as Totten reveals below.

"The wig…seemed placed to hide other features of the head"

"Second, her facial features: Though I could not see her eyes due to the large Jackie-O style sunglasses she wore, other aspects were evident: an unusually long pointy chin. Exaggerated cheekbones out of proportion to the rest of the face. Practically no lips, only enough to discern that there was any mouth. A nose that was almost not there: there was very little structure to it, a small bridge area, and some structure around the nostrils, but not much.

"Finally, her neck: though her coat collar was turned up, I could see some of the neck which was oddly thin. The wig (obviously such: a long thick dishwater blonde mane made of cheap imitation hair easily obtainable at a k-mart in those days) seemed placed to hide other features of the head, so I cannot comment on these (ears, shape of head).

"It puzzles me why I cannot recall her hand. Perhaps because it was what most startled me at first. The only thing I can relate to this lack of recall is a nasty car accident I had years later: afterwards I completely blanked out the memory of the worst part of the accident (the part when it was occurring). I asked my doctor about this and was told that it was not uncommon for the human brain to 'forget' traumatic or difficult events. I can only surmise the initial part of the encounter with the cigarette lady falls into this category.

"There were no other people in the store. I was alone. It was afternoon. The year of this encounter was 1974, possibly 1975 (I worked both summers between high school and college, and between my 1st and 2nd years of college); but most likely 1974. The location was an area south of St. Louis, Missouri.

"I felt no lingering psychological effect from this encounter that I am aware of, other than extreme puzzlement (and the blocked memory of her hand). As to whether this changed me, I don't know."

In many respects, the WIB that Karen Totten encountered sounds, from her description, astonishingly like the one encountered just a few years earlier, in Florida, by White House employee, Shirley Cromartie. As well as one that was accompanied by a strange man, and encountered in 1987 by a leading figure in the world of New York book-publishing, as will later be revealed.

Aliens or ancient humanoids?

Before his tragic and untimely death in 2009 at the age of just thirty-four, Mac Tonnies took a deep interest in the 1970s-era experience of Karen Totten. He did so in decidedly alternative fashion. Like Jacques Vallee and John Keel, Tonnies rightly recognized that UFO encounters cannot be dismissed as the ravings of lunatics, the tales of the fantasy-prone, or the fabrications of those seeking fame and fortune. But, he was also careful not to get sucked into the near-viral mindset that practically screams (take a deep breath): UFOs = alien spaceships piloted by little gray chaps from across the galaxy, who are on a mission to save their dying race by stealing our DNA, eggs and sperm.

Rather, Tonnies was chasing down the theory suggesting that the UFOnauts may actually represent the last vestiges of a very ancient race of distinctly *terrestrial* origins; a race that - tens of thousands of years ago - may have ruled our planet, but whose position of power was thrown into overwhelming chaos by two things; (A) the appearance of a "debilitating genetic syndrome" that ravaged their society; and (B) the rising infestation of a violent species that threatened to eclipse - in number - their own society. They are the Cryptoterrestrials, as Tonnies termed them. And that violent species that blusters around like an insane, unruly and spoiled child, and that has done more damage in its short life-time than can ever be truly imagined, is, of course, us.

"They quietly retreated into the shadows"

With their society waning, their health and ability to even successfully reproduce collapsing, and their absolute worst nightmare - the Human Race - becoming the new gang in town, the Cryptoterrestrials followed what was perceived as the only viable option: they quietly retreated into the shadows, into the darkened corners of our world, below the oceans, into the deepest caverns that pepper the planet, and in their own uniquely silent and detached way, set about a new course of action.

That course of action - given that they were in some fashion genetically related to the Human Race - was to eventually resurface; to move amongst us in stealth; to pass themselves off as entities from far-off worlds (as part of a concerted effort to protect and hide their real point of origin); and to use and exploit us - medically - in an attempt to try and inject their waning species with a considerable amount of new blood. *Ours*.

In addition, Tonnies believed, the Cryptoterrestrials were - and, by definition, still are - subtle-yet-brilliant, cosmic magicians. For them, however, there is no top hat from which a white-rabbit is pulled. There is no hot chick sliced in half and then miraculously rejoined at the waist. No: their tricks are far more fantastic. As well as deceiving us about their origins, the Cryptoterrestrials have - via, perhaps, the use of advanced hologram-style technology, mind-manipulation and much more - led us to conclude that they have an infinite number of craft, resources and technologies at their disposal.

And that is the trick, the ruse: in actuality, their numbers today, Tonnies strongly suspected, may be very small. They may well be staging faked UFO events to try and convince us that they have a veritable armada at their disposal when, perhaps, the exact opposite is the case. And, most important of all, they desperately want us to think of them as visitors from the stars. If their plan to rejuvenate their species is to work, then stealth, subterfuge and camouflage are the essential orders of the day.

"'Aliens' seem to spend a significant amount of time ensuring they are seen"

Of course, the above all amounts to a theory - just like the extrarerstrial hypothesis. And, Tonnies made it very clear that he *was* theorizing, rather than being able to provide the reader with definitive proof for such a scenario. He did, however, offer a logical, and at times powerful, argument in support of his theories.

As for so-called "alien abductions," the clumsy, intrusive means by which ova and sperm are taken by a race of beings we are led to believe are countless years ahead of us was also addressed by Tonnies. As was the unlikely scenario that our DNA would even be compatible, in the first place, with extraterrestrial entities. Tonnies' tentative conclusion: all this points not to the presence of highly-advanced aliens who are thousands of years ahead of us; but to the actions of an ancient Earth-based society whose technology may not be more than a century or so in advance of our current knowledge.

Tonnies also noted how the "aliens" seem to spend a significant amount of time ensuring they are seen: whether it's taking "soil-samples" at the side of the road; equipping their craft with bright, flashing lights; or hammering home the point to the abductees that they are from this planet, from that star-system, or from some far off galaxy. Just about anywhere and everywhere aside from right here, in fact.

Roswell came into Tonnies' equation, too: and in ingenious fashion. Those who do *not* adhere to the extraterrestrial hypothesis for Roswell point to the fact that many of the witness descriptions of what was found at Roswell, *are* collectively suggestive of some form of large balloon-type structure having come down at the Foster Ranch, Lincoln

County, New Mexico on that fateful day in the summer of 1947.

The possibility that ET would be flying around New Mexico in a balloon is absurd. But, as Tonnies noted, a race of impoverished, underground-dwellers, highly worried by the sudden influx of military activity in New Mexico (such as at the White Sands Proving Ground, and the Los Alamos Laboratory), just *might* employ the use of an advance balloon-type vehicle to secretly scope out the area late at night. Perhaps, when elements of the U.S. military came across the debris, they really *did* assume it was balloon-borne material and probably of American origin. Until, maybe, they stumbled across something else amid the debris, too: curious bodies; dead cryptoterrestrials.

Tonnies' theorizing continued in a similar vein. To the extent that we are left with a stark and surreal image of a very ancient - and very strange - race of beings who may once have been the masters of this planet; who were sidelined thousands of years ago; and who are now - under cover of darkness and while the cities sleep - forced to grudgingly surface from their darkened lairs and interact with the very things they fear (and perhaps even hate and despise) most of all.

That's us. Survival is the name of their game. And deception is the means by which it is being cunningly achieved. And, in Mac Tonnies' mind, Karen Totten's WIB just might have been one of those deceptive dwellers of the underground. Perhaps the answers to the mystery of the Women in Black will not be found within the stars above us, but in a mysterious realm far below us.

9

"The sky is very clear tonight"

Now let's head to the night of Saturday, September 11, 1976. That was the decidedly ill-fated evening upon which the Orchard Beach, Maine, home of a certain Dr. Herbert Hopkins was darkened by a nightmarish MIB – an event that was soon followed by the appearance of a very odd woman. Vampire-like scarcely begins to describe the terrible thing that descended on Hopkins' home on that fraught night. When Hopkins opened the front door, he was confronted by a pale-faced, skinny, bald ghoul; one that was dressed in black, had dark and hostility-filled eyes, and sported the de rigueur Fedora hat.

The MIB made it very clear, and extremely quickly, that if Hopkins knew what was good for him he would immediately cease all of his then-current research into the life and experiences of a reported alien abductee: David Stephens, who lived in nearby Oxford. Hopkins, frozen to the bone, didn't need telling twice. Just for good measure, the undeniably malevolent MIB – in monotone fashion – told Hopkins to take out of the right pocket of his pants one of the two coins that was in there and hold it in the open palm of his hand. Hopkins didn't even think to wonder how the MIB knew the coins were there; he just did as he was told.

With a detectable threat in his robotic voice, the MIB ordered Hopkins to keep his eyes locked on the coin, which he did. To Hopkins' amazement and horror, something terrifying happened: the coin transmuted. It turned blue in color; it shimmered slightly – as if in a mini heat-haze – and then, in a second or so, became 100 percent vaporous. After a few moments the vapor was gone. The MIB implied that he could do exactly the same thing to Hopkins' heart. Hopkins got the message. The MIB shuffled his curious way to the door and vanished – as in *literally* – into the chilled night. Hopkins' Man in Black sounds like one of the strange and enigmatic characters that, hundreds of years ago, turned up late at night, dressed in black, and who threatened early alchemists to leave the matter alone.

And, on this very point, there is one important thing I have left until now, something which further amplifies the connection between Herbert Hopkins' MIB and the alchemists of old. According to Hopkins, at one point the man touched his finger to his lips – deliberately, for effect, it seems. Although the man's face and hands were utterly white, his lips were bright red. When the MIB removed his finger from his lips, it was stained red. This led Hopkins to suspect the man, rather oddly and unsettlingly, was wearing lipstick. On the other hand, it's worth noting that, way back in the 17th century, one Wenzel Seiler's exposure to the domain of alchemy occurred when he ran his finger across a large, oak table in the monastery in which he worked, and found it coated in a bright red substance. It was, supposedly, the enigmatic Philosopher's Stone; the "key" to opening the "door" behind which the secrets of alchemy are said to be held. It was almost as if Herbert Hopkins' MIB was playing some very strange mind-game with Hopkins, ones in which he dropped more than a few clues to his – the MIB's – linkage to alchemy, the Philosopher's Stone, and the transmutation of coins.

The creepiest couple of all

It's almost no coincidence that thirteen days after Dr. Hopkins' experience, his eldest son, John, and his – John's – wife, Maureen, had a strange experience with what may well have been a WIB *and* a MIB. It was around 7:30 p.m. when Maureen took a very unusual phone call in the family home. Like so many calls from the MIB and the WIB, this one was filled with crackling and buzzing on the line, distortion, and a very strange and confusing conversation. The caller claimed to be a "Bill Post" from Conway, New Hampshire, who, supposedly, was a friend of an unnamed friend of John's. Post made it clear to Maureen that he and a companion wished to meet with both her and John – something that puzzled Maureen, not surprisingly.

John, rather oddly, agreed to drive out to a local McDonald's, where Post and his companion arranged to meet him – even though John had no idea of who the man was or what he wanted. Red flags were going up and alarm bells were ringing when John arrived: while Post claimed to hail from New Hampshire, the plates on his vehicle read "Temporary, N.J., 1975." On top of that, as John instructed the pair to follow him to his and Maureen's home, Post actually took a short cut, demonstrating that he was very familiar with the neighborhood and the roads, and was clearly *not* the out-of-towner he claimed to be. Both vehicles pulled up and John exited his, as Post and a still-unidentified woman got out of their car. They followed him into the house, and that's when things got really weird.

Post and the woman, who was introduced as "Jane," sat down and an awkward and weird situation unfolded. This was hardly surprising, since Bill Post and Jane – if those were their real names, which seems *most* unlikely – were hardly your average, every day visitors. Although, at first glance, they looked like regular people, there was something about them that was just not quite right; something hard to define, but something most definitely menacing and unsettling.

The man, estimated by John and Maureen to have been in his mid-thirties, had an extremely high-pitched voice, hair that was slicked down in an old style, and ears that were positioned very far back on the side of his head. As for Jane, she too appeared to be in her thirties, *also* had ears that were described as being "set well back," and had a "whining" quality to her voice. Not only that, she was wearing bright red lipstick very similar to that Herbert Hopkins' MIB seemingly wore just two weeks earlier, and her clothing was described as being decades out of date – something that absolutely typifies the MIB. There was something else, too, that neither Maureen nor John could fail to note: both the man and woman walked in a very weird way – they shuffled along and leaned significantly forward as they did so. "Surreal" scarcely begins to describe the decidedly off the wall situation.

John offered the pair Cokes, which they accepted but failed to even take a sip of – which is typical MIB/WIB behavior. For the most part, food and drink seems to confuse them. Then, things were taken to a whole new level: Post began to fondle Jane in front of John and Maureen, asking if he was "doing it right." Hardly surprisingly, it wasn't long at all before the conversation was brought to a close and Post and Jane stood up, shuffled out of the room and the front-door, and were gone, and all without even a single "goodbye."

It has been suggested that John and Maureen were swingers and that this was simply a case of a planned liaison, and a bit of late-night fun, gone awkwardly and embarrassingly wrong. And that, perhaps, Post and Jane had been referred to John and Maureen by friends in the swinging community. Regardless of whether or not John and Maureen engaged in something as harmless as swinging, there are several factors that lead one to believe that an anticipated evening of sexual fun was not the root-cause of this curious story. Let's take a look at a couple of aspects of the story that I have left untouched, until now.

First, the only reason why the story ever surfaced was because John chose to share it with his father, as John felt there was possibly a connection between the odd pair and Herbert Hopkins' equally odd MIB of two weeks earlier. Moreover, if the whole thing was down to nothing stranger than a swinging encounter that ended up not swinging in the slightest, why should John have even mentioned it to his father, Dr. Hopkins, in the first place? Second, there is the matter of the out of date clothes and hairstyles, the weird tonal qualities in the voices of the pair, their oddly positioned ears, their deliberate avoidance of drinks, and their curious shuffling gait – all of which can be found in countless WIB and MIB reports. Third, David Jacobs has noted that in the cases of alien-human hybridization that he has investigated, the hybrids seem confused by sex – to the point they sometimes act in fashions that some might find inappropriate. Just like the odd pair that freaked out John and Maureen.

"The sky is very clear tonight"

There was something else, too. Post repeatedly asked John how often he spoke with his father, and practically demanded to know what subjects they discussed. John was convinced that Post was digging for data and comments on his father's recent MIB experience. Then, quite out of the blue, Post said to John: "The sky is very clear tonight. You are going to be in amateur radio."

It transpired that Herbert Hopkins was a ham-radio enthusiast, but how Post apparently knew of the family's links to the subject utterly baffled John. As for the odd comment about the sky being clear, John pondered on the possibility that Post was implying tonight might be a very good night to see a UFO. Put all of that together and what one gets is hardly the image of a swinging good, or even bad, time on a Friday night behind closed doors, but something far more chilling – and something connected to Dr. Herbert Hopkins' encounter of two weeks previously.

Finally, John told his father that he couldn't fathom why he had agreed to go and meet Post and have him and his companion, Jane, follow him home – never mind let them into his and Maureen's home. Yet, we see this time and again: in both WIB and MIB encounters, the black-garbed ones seemingly have the ability to control or manipulate our minds and our common-sense factors to incredible degrees. The story of the White House's Shirley Cromartie being a classic example.

Of only one thing were John and Maureen certain: the encounter with "Bill Post" and "Jane" left them scared, confused, and more than a bit paranoid – which, quite possibly, was the specific goal of the whole experience. Namely, to intimidate the pair and ensure that word got back to Dr. Hopkins, thus plunging him into an even deeper state of anxiety. Few will be surprised to know that is *precisely* what happened.

With that all said, it's time for us to take a detour and dig a bit deeper into matters alchemical and links to the WIB and MIB.

<u>10</u>

"They wore long black cloaks"

Brad Steiger, who has a particular fascination for alchemy, says: "Helvetius, the grandfather of the celebrated philosopher of the same name, was an alchemist who labored ceaselessly to fathom the mystery of the 'philosopher's stone,' the legendary catalyst that would transmute base metals into gold. One day in 1666 when he was working in his laboratory at the Hague, a stranger attired all in black, as befitted a respectable burgher of North Holland, appeared and informed him that he would remove all the alchemist's doubts about the existence of the philosopher's stone, for he himself possessed such an object."

In 1852, Charles Mackay wrote of this affair that the Man in Black "…asked Helvetius if he thought he should know that rare gem if he saw it. To which Helvetius replied, that he certainly should not. The burgher immediately drew from his pocket a small ivory box, containing three pieces of metal, of the color of brimstone, and extremely heavy; and assured Helvetius, that of them he could make as much as twenty tons of gold. Helvetius informs us, that he examined them very attentively; and seeing that they were very brittle, he took the opportunity to scrape off a small portion with his thumb-nail. He then returned to the stranger, with an entreaty that he would perform the process of transmutation before him. The stranger replied, that he was not allowed to do so, and went away."

Mackay continued that several weeks later the mysterious character in black was back. Helvetius implored the MIB to share with him the secrets of alchemy, which, apparently, he did: "Helvetius repeated the experiment alone, and converted six ounces of lead into very pure gold."

Such was the fame that surrounded this event, said Mackay, "all of the notable persons of the town flocked to the study of Helvetius to convince themselves of the fact. Helvetius performed the experiment again, in the presence of the Prince of Orange, and several times afterwards, until he exhausted the whole of the powder he had received from the stranger, from whom it is necessary to state, he never received another visit; nor did he ever discover his name or condition."

Just like every WIB and MIB, Helvetius' Man in Black forever remained an elusive enigma.

A black-garbed manipulator of metal

In 1677, Leopold I, the Holy Roman Emperor and King of Austria, suffered something terrible: his precious supply of gold finally became exhausted. This was utterly disastrous, as it was gold, specifically, that Leopold relied upon to pay his troops, as they sought to keep at bay the marauding attacks of the Turks. Help, however, was soon at hand, and in a decidedly curious fashion.

Late one night, in November 1672, Leopold was visited by a monk of the Order of St. Augustine, one Johann Wenzel Seiler. Interestingly, it has been suggested that "Johann Wenzel Seiler" was actually a pseudonym that the dark-garbed, cloaked, and hooded character had adopted. Whatever the truth, Seiler confidently said he could banish all of the king's problems in an instant. The king, who already had an interest in all-things-alchemical, listened carefully to what Seiler had to say.

The monk motioned Leopold to follow him to the steps of the palace, which he did. It was on the steps that Seiler did something remarkable. He took a silver medallion, placed into a cauldron of magical liquid, and then extracted it. Lo and behold, it had been transformed into gold. The king was delighted, Austria's gold problem (or, rather, the sudden lack of it) was solved.

In 1880, Dr. Franz Hartmann, who carefully and deeply studied the controversy surrounding alchemy, said: "...it is stated that this medal, consisting originally of silver, has been partly transformed into gold, by alchemical means, by the same Wenzel Seiler who was afterwards made a knight by the Emperor Leopold I and given the title Wenzeslaus Ritter von Reinburg."

Alchemy: a particular fascination of the WIB and the MIB
(Joseph Wright, 1771).

Interestingly, Hartmann pointed out that many came
to believe Seiler was not who he claimed to be, and was
soon "regarded as an impostor." Specifically, this was with
regard to claims that Seiler had merely coated the medallion

with a gold-colored substance, rather than having literally transformed it into gold. Nevertheless, and despite exiling Seiler shortly afterwards, Leopold – seemingly entranced by Seiler, as are so many that encounter the WIB and the MIB – continued to eagerly employ the skills of this mysterious character, time and again.

"Nobody can identify that coin"

Moving on to the 1950s, there is the following story – of a curious coin and a trio of MIB – that reached the eyes and ears of a variety of 1950s-era UFO researchers, including Morris Jessup and Gray Barker, as well as a science-fiction author named Donald A. Wollheim, who sometimes used the pseudonym of David Grinnell. That it's a story with a link to both the MIB and to the world of alchemy is something which requires us to take note of it, the reason being that the author of the story – seemingly for no apparent reason – made a specific point of noting to Morris Jessup that he was deeply interested in the domain of alchemy.

Since the story is an important one, I have related it, below, without interruption:

"I cannot say whether I am the victim of a very ingenious jest on the part of some of my wackier friends or whether I am just someone accidentally 'in' in some top-secret business. But it happened, and it happened to me personally, while visiting Washington recently, just rubber-necking, you know, looking at the Capitol and the rest of the big white buildings.

"It was summer, fairly hot. Congress was not in session, nothing much was doing, most people vacationing. I was that day aiming to pay a visit to the State Department, not knowing that I couldn't, for there was nothing public to see there unless it's the imposing and rather martial lobby (it used to be the War Department building, I'm told). This I did not find out until I had blithely walked up the marble steps to the entrance, passed the big bronze doors, and wandered about in the huge lobby, wherein a small number of people, doubtless on important business, were passing in and out.

"A guard, sitting near the elevators, made as if to start in my direction to find out whom and what the deuce I wanted, when one of the elevators came down and a group of men hustled out. There were two men, evidently State Department escorts, neatly clad in gray double-breasted suits, with three other men walking with them. The three men struck me as a little odd; they wore long black cloaks, big slouch hats with wide brims pulled down over their faces, and carried portfolios. They looked for all the world like cartoon representations of cloak-and-dagger spies. I supposed that they were some sort of foreign diplomats and, as they were coming directly toward me, stood my ground, determined to see who they were.

"The floor was marble and highly polished. One of the men nearing me suddenly seemed to lose his balance. He slipped: his feet shot out from under him, and he fell. His portfolio slid directly at my feet.

"Being closest to him, I scooped up the folio and was the first to help raise him to his feet. Grasping his arm, I hoisted him from the floor – he seemed to be astonishingly weak in the legs; I felt almost that he was about to topple again. His companions stood about rather flustered, helplessly, their faces curiously impassive. And though the man I helped must have received a severe jolt, his face never altered expression.

"Just then the two State Department men recovered their own poise, rushed about, and, getting between me and the man I had rescued, rudely brushed me aside, and rushed their party to the door.

"Now what bothers me is not the impression I got that the arm beneath that man's sleeve was curiously woolly, as if he had a fur coat underneath the cloak (and this in a Washington summer!), and it's not the impression that he was wearing a mask (the elastic band of which I distinctly remember seeing amidst the kinky, red, close-cropped hair of his head). No, it's not that at all, which might be momentarily misconstructions on my part. It's the coin that I picked up off the floor where he'd dropped his portfolio.

"I've searched through every stamp and coin catalogue I can find or borrow, and I've made inquiries of a dozen language teachers and professors, and nobody can identify that coin or the lettering around its circumference.

"It's about the size of a quarter, silvery, very light in weight, but also very hard. Besides the lettering on it, which even the Bible Society, which knows a thousand languages and dialects, cannot decipher, there is a picture on one side and a symbol on the other.

"The picture is the face of a man, but a man with very curiously wolfish features: sharp canine teeth parted in what could be called a smile; a flattened, broad, and somewhat protruding nose, more like a pug dog's muzzle; sharp, widely spaced vulpine eyes; and definitely hairy and pointed ears.

"The symbol on the other side is a circle with latitude and longitude lines on it. Flanking the circle, one on each side, are two crescent-shaped moons."

That the unknown letter writer (A) made a point to Morris Jessup of stressing his interest in alchemy; (B) spent more than several lines describing the curious, silver coin; and (C) tied all of this in with the Men in Black, provokes an intriguing possibility: that the man was deliberately trying to tell people of the connection between the MIB and the domain of ancient alchemical experimentation.

And, finally, there is one more, strange tale concerning the WIB and coins. Gerry Armstrong, of Jackson's Point, Canada, was someone who had a bizarre experience in a record store in the town's Newport Plaza back in October 1973. According to Armstrong, he was served by "the most beautiful girl I had ever seen." She wore a long and flowing black dress, had long, coal-black hair, and possessed what

Armstrong called, "the blackest eyes I had ever seen." Most mysterious of all, after Armstrong paid for the old, vinyl LPs, the WIB threw his change – *coins* – onto the floor and literally vanished. Not without significance, at the time, Armstrong was having a significant number of UFO encounters.

11

"Rambling wolves seeking whom they can devour"

The 1980s saw a deeply disturbing and even dangerous development in the saga of the Women in Black. In fact, it was just about the most disturbing and dangerous development of all. It revolved around the phenomenon of what became infamously known as "Phantom Social Workers" (PSW) or "Bogus Social Workers" (BSW). On numerous occasions, terrified parents throughout the United Kingdom were plagued by visits to their homes from pale- or tanned-skinned, black-garbed women – occasionally accompanied by men – who claimed they were there to investigate reports of abuse to babies and children, whether mental, physical, or sexual. In many such cases, the claimed social workers acted in extremely strange and unsettling fashions, and created atmospheres filled with dread and high-strangeness. Not only that, a significant number of the reports eerily paralleled the saga of the so-called female "census takers" of the 1960s, which so fascinated and unsettled the mind of John Keel.

To detail all of the many and varied cases on record would require an entire book on the subject alone. A study of a number of stand-out cases, however, will demonstrate the nature of the events. But, before doing so, it's important I do something that no other previous commentator on this particular issue has done before. Namely, to demonstrate that the connection between the WIB and children is nothing new. The media of both the U.K. and Canada was reporting on such particularly disturbing issues more than a *century* ago. So, with that said, let's begin with the past and then, in the next chapter, head to the 1980s and the present day.

"She was spoken of as the 'Lady in Black'"

A very macabre story, involving a Woman in Black and a newborn baby – both of who subsequently vanished – was published in the October 31, 1891 edition of the Hull, England *Weekly Mail* newspaper. That's right: it appeared on Halloween, the most bone-chilling night of the year. The night on which it is said the veil between the land of the living and the domain of the dead is at its absolute thinnest. The title of the article was concise and to the point: "The Lady In Black."

It was the kind of affair that would have been ideal for Sherlock Holmes to have gotten his teeth into, given that the exploits of the world's most famous, fictional detective were riding high at the time. The feature began as follows:

"A strange case of supposed kidnapping is reported from Hull. It seems, as the story goes at present, that a woman named Proctor, wife of a laboring man, with a family of six children, on Wednesday night committed her infant, nine days old, to the care of a relative, Mrs. Dryer, to be baptized at St. Andrew's Church."

The story continued: "Accompanying Mrs. Dryer was an elderly woman, who had been visiting Mrs. Proctor, and who had shown her sympathy in a practical form."

And then things got a bit more mysterious: "Her name or whence she came was unknown to the household or in the neighborhood, except that she was spoken of as the 'Lady in Black,' and was supposed to be a district visitor."

What began as a mysterious story quickly became one of sinister proportions: "They arrived at the church too late for the ceremony to take place. Mrs. Dryer, it is stated, gave the infant to her companion while she went outside for a moment. On her return the woman and child were gone."

"Sinister" soon gave way to "terrifying," as the local media noted: "Late the same evening the infant's clothes were found in a street nearby with a note attached, stating, 'Baby is all right. Baby and I have gone to Leeds.' There was no signature to this strange communication. No trace has yet been found of either woman or child."

Nor was any trace ever found. The Woman in Black and the stolen baby were gone. *Forever.*

"A woman of medium height, dressed in black
and wearing a cape, was seen strolling along
Kintyre Avenue"

Seven years later, there was yet another strange story involving a newborn baby and a Woman in Black. This time, however, the location was Toronto, Canada. The *Daily Mail and Empire* newspaper reported (in an article titled "Woman in Black"), on April 7, 1898, that an approximately six-day-old baby had been found abandoned on the doorstep of a Mr. Eli G. Roselin, a carpenter, of 65 Grant Street, Toronto. It was very fortunate for the baby that Roselin worked late that night. As he reached his home around 9:00 p.m., he saw a small bundle on the doorstep. It contained, to his astonishment and shock, a small baby, one who had been, it was later determined, "dosed with drugs and whisky." Police were quickly alerted and the baby was taken to the local "Infants Home."

Newspaper staff noted that: "Investigation last night established the fact pretty conclusively that the child had been placed on the step not more than twenty minutes before it was found. The spot is a rather lonely one, opposite Kintyre Avenue, and there are half a dozen ways of approach and escape from the locality."

And, then, there was this: "A woman of medium height, dressed in black and wearing a cape, was seen strolling along Kintyre Avenue from 8 to 8.30 o'clock, by some boys, by a lady living on Grant Street, and by Mr. Farmery, of 63 Grant Street. She had something concealed under her cape, and it is believed by the neighbors that she may have left the child on the step. Mr. Joselin's bell was not rung when the infant was abandoned."

There's also the matter of whether the baby was that of the caped Woman in Black, or if the WIB had kidnapped the baby in a fashion not unlike the situation that occurred in Hull, England in 1891.

"It just struck me as something out of this world"

There is a *very* curious afterword to this story. More than a century later, the mummified remains of a baby were found on none other than the above-mentioned spot, nearby Kintyre Avenue. They were wrapped in a tattered and torn edition of the *Mail and Empire* newspaper, the very newspaper that reported on a Woman in Black and a dumped baby, back in 1898. In a September 24, 2007 article for the Toronto *Star*, titled "Does mummified baby have living cousin?" Francine Kopun, who wrote the article, noted the following:

"Rita Rich was 10 years old in 1925 when someone buried a newborn baby beneath the floorboards of the house where she lived with her father and her aunt and uncle, at 29 Kintyre Ave. in Toronto. She was as shocked as anyone to learn, 82 years after the fact, that she had lived for years with the remains of an infant boy beneath her feet. His mummified corpse was discovered by a renovator working on the house in July. The baby was curled in the fetal position and wrapped in a comforter and a *Mail and Empire* newspaper dated Sept. 15, 1925.

"'It just struck me as something out of this world,' says Rich, now 92 and living in Medina, an Erie Canal village in Western New York State. 'I wondered how it could happen and I wouldn't know it.'

"An autopsy concluded the infant had no broken bones or evidence of other injuries. Testing on the air sacs in his lungs revealed that he was likely born alive, although the findings were not conclusive, according to Toronto Deputy Chief Coroner Dr. Jim Cairns. No cause of death could be established."

In early October 2007, the remains of the baby were laid to rest in Toronto's Elgin Mills Cemetery. The case still remains unresolved.

"She was a thin, dark woman, dressed in black"
- -

Moving on, it's now time to turn our attentions to the Bromley, Kent, England, *Evening Express* newspaper. In its May 16, 1910 issue, there appeared an article titled "Mysterious Lady In Black." The article began in appropriately uncanny and unsettling style: "Coming from apparently nowhere and vanishing mysteriously, an unknown woman attended at a birth in Stepney, and at the inquest, although the coroner tried to elucidate the mystery, he was unable to do so."

The unnamed journalist who wrote the small article added that the baby in question was Elizabeth McDonald, who tragically died just five days after her birth. She was said to have been the daughter of "a seaman, of Eastward Street, Bromley." The story continued that one of those present at the birth was a woman, a widow, named Elizabeth Dowsett. After poor, soon-to-be-doomed Elizabeth was born, Dowsett went to the second-floor room to see the newborn baby and was followed by a woman who "came into the room and did all that was necessary."

In light of that, the coroner asked: "Do you mean that some stranger went up the stairs behind you, and did all this, and you don't know who she was?"

Dowsett replied quickly and said something that, by now, will be chillingly familiar: "I had never seen her before. She was a thin, dark woman, dressed in black."

The coroner continued: "You can tell us a lot more about this mysterious lady in black, if you like. What became of her afterwards?"

"I don't know," admitted Dowsett.

"What? Did she drop from the clouds and then vanish into thin air?" asked the coroner, amazed. Given that the WIB – just like the MIB – have an uncanny knack of disappearing in the blink of an eye, the coroner may have been closer to the truth than he could ever have possibly imagined.

Dowsett could only offer a speculative answer: "She went out the same way she came in, I expect."

These "I expect" words are important because they make it clear Dowsett had no real clue as to what happened to the Woman in Black – at all. The death of little Elizabeth, said one Dr. Meadows, was due to "syncope," an antiquated term for loss of consciousness, fainting, or "swooning." It's a condition that a person usually recovers from quickly. But not Elizabeth McDonald, unfortunately.

Perhaps with some justification, the coroner said to Dowsett that she should keep her doors firmly locked at night, due to the apparent presence of "some rambling wolves about seeking whom they can devour." Quite.

"The man and woman took Susie away"

Moving onto 1909, a very disturbing set of circumstances that occurred in Barnet, Hertfordshire, England, in that year. The story was spelled out in an article sub-titled "Pauper Child Kidnapped" which appeared in the pages of the *Nottingham Evening Post*. As for the title of the article, it was concise and to the point: "The Woman in Black."

It reported how a nine-year-old girl named Susan Smith had been kidnapped under "extraordinary circumstances." According to Susan's school-friends, she was taken away by a "dirty and rough-looking man" and a woman "dressed in black."

One of Susan's friends, Rose Armitage, said: "When Susie and I came out of school there was a man and a woman standing on the other side of the road. They called to Susan, and she said, 'That's my mother.' But she didn't want to go with them. The woman gave Susie a jam tart, but she wouldn't eat it. So I ate it instead. Then the man and woman took Susie away with them down the road."

The story continued that Susan had "led a wandering existence, and there are at least three women whom she calls mother, so no importance can be attached to her remark, 'that's my mother.'"

In view of that, it's not impossible this was some sort of domestic affair. However, as will now become apparent, the story of Susan Smith has its parallels with events that began in the U.K. in the 1980s. And particularly so cases where a man and a woman were present at the time of the attempted kidnap.

12

"We would urge everyone to be vigilant"

Of one classic, early case of the modern era, investigator Peter Rogerson said the following, which accurately and concisely demonstrates the nature of the phenomenon, and of the Bogus Social Worker/Phantom Social Worker and their modus operandi:

"A woman described as being her late 20s, 5'7" (1.7m) in height, blonde, wearing a brown skirt suit, a white polo neck and carrying a briefcase called to a house near Blessington, Co. Wicklow, Ireland, claiming that she was a Public Health Nurse who had to take a baby boy away for vaccinations. She knew the boy's name and date of birth, but when the mother requested identification, the BSW upped sticks and left. The Eastern Health Board has issued warnings following the incident, advising people to be vigilant."

The reason why the authorities urged such vigilance was because the wave of BSW reports followed in the immediate wake of a "satanic abuse" scare that exploded across much of the U.K., including Rochdale, Nottingham, and Manchester. There were outlandish tales of babies being sacrificed, and even eaten, in abominable rituals to Satan and his demonic minions. Tales of aborted fetuses used in similar infernal rites, in darkened woods, and at the witching-hour, abounded too. Major inquiries were launched, but nothing ever surfaced to suggest the hysterical rumors were anything other than that: hysterical rumors. It's hardly surprising, though, that the public and government agencies – and particularly so the police – were on edge.

"Vaguely menacing strangers"

Patrick Harpur, the author of an excellent piece of work, *Daimonic Reality*, commented on a wave of BSW activity that broke out in the U.K. in 1990. Of these emotionless characters, who Harpur described as "vaguely menacing strangers who turn up in the vicinity of nefarious goings-on, but who are unfailingly ineffective," he said:

"Reports poured in to the police, describing 'health workers' or 'social workers' who called to examine or take away children, but who hurriedly left when the householder became suspicious. The visitors were mostly one or two women, but sometimes a woman and a man. The women were typically in their late twenties or early thirties, heavily made up, smartly dressed and of medium height. They carried clipboards and, often, identification cards."

Harpur continued that by May 1990, the reports had

grown in such numbers that the police believed no less than four groups of people were at work. He added: "They were thought to be gangs of pedophiles. But clearly there were signs that the matter was far from straightforward: the pedophile theory was weakened by the involvement of so many women, who are rarely implicated in pedophilia (except in cases of alleged satanic ritual abuse)."

"The social workers beat a diplomatic retreat"

Mike Dash, who has made a noteworthy contribution to the Bogus Social Worker controversy, has investigated yet another report from 1990; this one involving a woman named Elizabeth Coupland, of Sheffield, England. It was a winter's day when two women knocked on Coupland's door. Dressed in a fashion that suggested authority, the pair identified themselves as coming from the National Society for the Prevention of Cruelty to Children (NSPCC). Such was their manipulative skill, Coupland allowed the pair in, and even let them examine her children – one aged two and the other not even yet six months old.

According to Mike Dash: "The visitors soon left, and Coupland assumed that she would hear nothing more of the matter." Coupland was wrong. Dead wrong. Dash notes that a couple of days later, one of the women returned. But this time with a man. Coupland was shell-shocked to learn that her children were to be taken away from her and to be placed into care. The terrified mother, now very suspicious, loudly said that she was going to call the police, at which point, says Dash, "…the social workers beat a diplomatic retreat." It's hardly surprising – but disturbing - that the real NSPCC knew nothing of this highly worrying state of affairs.

Dash adds that these mysterious women have "continued to knock on the doors the length and breadth of Britain. They were in Edinburgh in 1995 and in Leicester a month later. They have called at homes in Bristol, Bath, Blackburn, Battersea and Barnsley." He observes, too, that not a single person has ever been charged in connection with any of these odd visits.

Dash notes one more thing: in the same way that in the United States the Women in Black and the MIB seemingly have a thing for old-style, black Cadillac cars, in the U.K. the Bogus Social Workers "displayed an inexplicable preference for driving red, A-registered Vauxhall Cavaliers."

ID of the bogus kind

Paul Meehan, who has researched the British BSW phenomenon, too, says: "A typical case occurred on the morning of October 10, 1995, when Mark Dunn was alone in his home in Manchester, his wife and children out of the house, and a visitor came to the door. It was a well-groomed, official looking woman of about 35, who claimed to be a social worker with the Manchester City Council investigating alleged mistreatment of his younger child. When Mr. Dunn demanded to see her identification, the woman told him she had to retrieve it from her car. Dunn observed her retreat to a parked car in which two men were waiting. The woman then got in and the car raced off."

Meehan adds: "Another BSW case occurred in Leigh, Lancashire, when a well-dressed couple came to the door of one Mrs. Carter, a local nurse who had two daughters. The man, who had the air of a petty bureaucrat, produced a photo ID that identified him as a worker with the community's social services department, while the woman wore a scarf emblazoned with the words, 'Child Protection.' The 'social workers' claimed they were there to investigate reports that Mrs. Carter was not feeding her children properly."

After the weird duo checked the family's food supplies – by obsessively ferreting through the pantry, no less – and demanded to physically examine the children, Mrs. Carter decided enough was well and truly enough and sent the pair packing. They got the hint and hurried out of the house – and into a large van parked outside. Somewhat ominously, it contained several others of their weird breed.

"A suspicious call"

In November 1996, a female BSW, accompanied by a man, surfaced in Limerick, Ireland. The pair showed up at the door of one particular home and demanded to be allowed to physically examine the family's four-year-old. One month later, County Cork, Ireland was hit by the BSW enigma. In the first case a man and a woman actually tried to abduct a 17-month-old child from her parents. Less than forty-eight hours later, it was at Blarney that a female BSW tried to force her way into the home of a couple that had a newborn baby. Fortunately, the baby-minder who was looking after the child, while the parents were at work, astutely realized there was something very suspicious about the woman and slammed the door on her. The BSW quickly vanished, never to be seen again.

And the cases have continued well into the 21st Century.

Five years later, in 2001, and in an article titled "Bogus Social Workers Hunt," the *Scottish Daily Record* reported the following: "Police were yesterday hunting two distinctively dressed bogus social workers who made a suspicious call at a house. The man and woman rushed off when challenged for identification at the property in Southside Road, Inverness, on Friday. Social work bosses said they had no staff in the area at the time. The man was described as 40 to 45, 5ft 10in tall, stockily [sic] built, with short ginger hair, goatee beard, wearing a green tweed sports jacket, check shirt, bright red tie, bottle green trousers and dark rectangular-framed glasses. The woman was 30 to 40, 5ft 6in, with shoulder-length brown hair, wearing a green coat and brown shoes and carrying a briefcase."

The reports continued to surface.

An on-going puzzle

Thirteen years down the line, in 2014, the U.K's *Daily Mail* was carefully following the apparently never-ending BSW affair. On April 25, the newspaper's Damien Gayle noted that: "Parents have been told to be vigilant after a bogus social worker called at a house and examined a baby. The woman, who claimed to be from Gloucestershire social services, tricked her way into the home in Quedgeley with fake ID and listened to the child's heartbeat with a stethoscope. She told the mother there were concerns for the welfare of her four-month-old son."

Detective Inspector Andy Dangerfield, of Gloucestershire Police, assured the press that the woman had at no time come into physical contact with the baby, but added: "We don't know what the motivation for this was but clearly it is very concerning. Our inquiries are ongoing. We have visited houses in the area to warn local people and would urge everyone to be vigilant. Remember, do not accept people into your house unless you are 100% sure you know who they are. You can always tell them to stay outside until you have made your own inquiries and if you are suspicious in any way, then call police. We have liaised with our partners at Gloucestershire social care services and they have alerted their staff to this incident."

What was particularly interesting about the woman who caused so much mental trauma for the family in question was her appearance. By now, it will be all too unsettlingly familiar. She was white, was estimated to have been in her late twenties or early thirties, was around 5-feet 6-inches tall, and had dark, shoulder-length hair. On top of that, she was dressed head to foot in a black trouser suit and had a "slightly tanned face."

It's almost certainly not mere coincidence that many of the cases involving Women in Black, female "census takers," and Men in Black that John Keel investigated in and around Point Pleasant, West Virginia, in the 1960s had noticeably tanned skin and were darkly garbed. One example, from spring 1967, is enough to hammer home the point: "Several local residents saw three very tall, dark complexioned men in the area. These men knocked on doors late at night, purportedly selling magazines. They spoke fluent unaccented English and were described as 'good-looking' with heavily tanned skin. Their height and broadness impressed the witnesses the most. These men were always on foot; apparently they did not have a car."

Note the ruse of "selling magazines," which was clearly a tactic to allow the tanned MIB to try and access the homes of those they visited. So, with a wealth of cases now highlighted, it's time to take a look at theories that have been suggested for the PSW/BSW phenomenon.

"The strangers who know everything"

Hardly surprising, is the fact that Britain's Police Force intensely investigated these potentially deadly events from the very beginning. They consistently came away baffled, however, which is not surprising and perhaps inevitable. Theories put forward by the police – from the 1980s and right up until 2014 - included potential burglars scoping out the properties; gangs of pedophiles; private detectives (possibly involved in marital disputes and child-custody cases); self-appointed child abuse vigilantes; psychologically damaged women whose children had died and who, while spiraling into the depths of mental illness, were trying to create new families; real social workers who overstepped the mark in terms of their approach; and even – bizarrely – gangs of visiting Mormons. None of the theories led any-where – other than in the direction of an unmoving, brick wall, that is.

Peter Rogerson notes, with a great deal of significance, the fact that the BSW are highly elusive – as Britain's police learned to their cost – and have a number of MIB-like parallels: "The stories of the 'phantom social workers,' the strangers who know everything, who appear out of nowhere and disappear after acting in a strange irrational manner, more than echo the motif of the Men in Black. None are caught, no car number plates are recorded. This kind of carry-on is not unknown - and perhaps not linked to child abuse. The BSWs are generally well-spoken, well dressed and well informed, especially of many personal details about their potential victims. Females BSWs seem to be the most common, but couples and the odd male are not unknown."

Bob Rickard, of *Fortean Times* magazine, noted yet another MIB parallel: "Like the enigmatic Men in Black of UFO fame, the BSWs are sometimes quite ignorant about those they have come to see; yet, at other times, they seem to know intimate details."

"Dr. Abner Mality" offers an intriguing theory, that the "...Phantom Social Workers, are 'tricksters'...beings that are 'playing games' with humanity. The famed paranormal writer John Keel, along with student of the bizarre Loren Coleman, have expressed the idea that much of what we call the paranormal and inexplicable is the result of these 'tricksters' playing with our perceptions. As to what their ultimate goal is, one can only speculate. Is it merely entertainment? Or is it some deeper purpose, perhaps preparing us to deal with the unknown? Sheer malevolence seems unlikely, as very few people have ever been actually harmed by these beings..."

Jeff Wells, of the *Rigorous Institution* blog, observes that the BSW stories, for Patrick Harpur, amount to "... the product of the daimonic imagination. Harpur goes so far as to suggest that the 'social workers' were themselves daimons: tricksters perpetrating practical jokes on the merely human and, like the so-called Men in Black, not doing any real harm."

Whatever the truth of the matter, the largely female BSW are undeniably as manipulative and fear-inducing as their MIB counterparts.

13

"I didn't want to get bitten"

In early 1987, a very bizarre incident - one that was, per-haps, supernaturally orchestrated - occurred at a Manhattan bookstore. It has undeniable parallels to the experiences of Truman Bethurum and Aura Rhanes in 1952, Shirley Cromartie in 1971, and Karen Totten in the mid-1970s. That's to say, it involved a woman who was heavily masked, hidden, camouflaged, who was clearly not human, and who left a deep, lasting impression on the witness. The woman was not alone, however. She had a male companion, as the WIB sometimes do. Particularly so in cases involving "bogus social-workers," and, as will be recalled, in the Aura Rhanes affair, too. The timeframe, the location, and the witness, are three of the most important aspects of the story, as will now become apparent.

It was a wintry, freezing, and dark Saturday afternoon in the latter part of January 1987 and a man named Bruce Lee - who worked as a senior editor at a New York pub-lishing house, William Morrow & Co. - walked into a bookstore on the Upper East Side of Manhattan. It was the now- closed-down Womrath's, on Lexington Avenue. Also with Lee was his wife.

It turns out that William Morrow & Co. had then very recently published Whitley Strieber's *New York Times'* bestseller, *Communion* – a book that told of Strieber's very own and deeply personal encounters of the so-called "alien abduction" variety. Womrath's had a large display set up for *Communion* and they also stocked a couple of Lee's own books. Quite naturally, Lee, who had also worked for *Reader's Digest* and *Newsweek*, was curious to see how both of the displays looked.

At this point, Lee and his wife parted and she headed off to the fiction section. Lee's attention was suddenly drawn to a strange couple that entered the store. In his own words, the pair headed "directly for *Communion*." He explained: "I mean, it was just, you could see them come in – they didn't know where the book was, you couldn't see it from the street – and they came in and headed right back for where that rack was. Most unusual, if you see what I mean."

Yes, we do.

That was not the only unusual thing about that fateful, Saturday afternoon. Both the man and the woman were barely five feet in height – maybe even slightly smaller. They had scarves that covered their chins, hats pulled tightly down, and huge, black sunglasses. They also appeared to begin speed-reading the book, noting out loud – one might even suggest for Lee's benefit – where Strieber had "got this wrong" and "got that wrong." They also giggled in a strange, unsettling fashion. We've seen that before, too.

Quite naturally, given that he worked for the very publisher that had just released *Communion*, Lee walked over and asked the pair what was wrong with the book. The woman suddenly looked up, at which point Lee was able to see through her sunglasses that her eyes were not just large, but huge, and shaped like almonds. Lee, by his own admission, felt the hackles on the back of his neck rise, and got a "mad dog" feeling emanating from the woman. He was likely not wrong when he observed: "I got to feeling that I was in eyeball contact with somebody who did not like me at all."

Such was the nature of the woman, Lee literally began to shake, backed away, quickly looked for his wife, and fled the store. "I didn't want to get bitten" he said.

Was the woman sending a message to Lee, one that was all but guaranteed to get back to both William Morrow & Co., and to Strieber himself? Very possibly, yes, since that's precisely what happened. Certainly, it hardly seems likely that this encounter between Bruce Lee and the "mad dog" woman, and her silent male partner, was down to nothing stranger than chance. Now, let's take a look at a certain Woman in Beige. She, too, has a connection to Whitley Strieber and his blockbuster, *Communion*.

"Every once in a while I think about that tall woman"

Two months after Bruce Lee's traumatic experience in Womrath's, there was yet another encounter in a bookstore that had at its heart a mysterious woman and Whitley Strieber's 1987 bestseller, *Communion*. In this case, the person in question was a psychoanalyst, Dr. Lee Zahner-Roloff. As he walked through the store, a tall, blond woman came towards him, holding in her arms – almost as one would cradle a newborn baby – a copy of *Communion*. Zahner-Roloff told Strieber: "In passing her I was overwhelmed with a sudden urge to pick up that book. Why would I pick up that book, about which I knew nothing, and seemed to have a loss of control regarding the purchase of?" He added that, "I lost personal volition completely."

Zahner-Roloff bought the book and quickly told work colleagues about it. In no time at all, it was as if an epidemic of alien-themed dreams took hold of him and his work friends. He said to Strieber: "Every once in a while I think about that tall woman in the beige suit carrying your book face forward through the aisles."

No doubt.

14

"This thing he is doing with UFOs, tell him to stop it, right away"

Throughout the summer and fall of 1997, the skies of south Devon, England were filled with UFOs, bizarre aerial vehicles, and mystifying lights. Strange creatures - including large black cats resembling mountain lions, flying beasts that had the appearance of huge jellyfish, and ghostly black dogs with blazing, hate-filled eyes – provoked terror in those that encountered them. Unidentified robed and hooded figures were seen prowling around local, dark woods by moonlight, seemingly engaging in infernal, occult-driven rites and rituals. Animals were found dead, and hideously mutilated, under mysterious circumstances.

Trying to make some sense of all this high-strangeness were two dedicated investigators of all things paranormal, Nigel Wright and Jon Downes. Wright is a well-known, long-time investigator of UFOs in England, while Downes is the director of the Devon-based Center for Fortean Zoology – one of the few groups that investigates reports of such anomalies as lake monsters, Bigfoot, and the Chupacabra on a full-time basis.

*Nigel Wright and Jon Downes, authors of The Rising
of the Moon (Nick Redfern, 1999).*

Such was the sheer scale of supernatural activity that
descended on ancient Devon in that specific period, Downes
and Wright found themselves plunged into a dark and turbulent world, one which closely paralleled the menacing
environment that threatened to swallow up John Keel, as
he investigated the turbulent Point Pleasant, West Virginia
Mothman reports of 1966-1967. And, in the same way that
Keel had run-ins with the MIB, both Downes and Wright
experienced something chillingly similar. For Downes, it
was hang-up phone calls in the middle of the night, and
confrontations with none other than representatives of

Britain's elite police unit, Special Branch – but for why, exactly, Downes was never told. As for Wright, well, he had the dubious pleasure of having one of our mysterious women on his tail.

It's important to note that Wright's case occurred when his research was at its absolute height. It was research that ultimately led to the publication of a book co-written with Downes on the 1997 wave. Its title, *The Rising of the Moon*. Not only that: at the same time Wright was also having regressing hypnotherapy to help him understand a suspected missing time/alien abduction experience in his childhood. As an example of Wright's research when south Devon was blighted by dark forces, consider the following.

"They turned the scene and fled"

Any mention of "animal mutilations" invariably, and quite understandably too, provokes imagery of the notorious "cattle-mutilation" events that reached their peak in the southwest regions of the United States in the mid to late 1970s. On the issue of whether or not the killing and mutilation of animals on a large scale was, and perhaps still is, the work of extraterrestrials, occult groups, government personnel engaged in biological warfare experimentation, scavengers, shadowy figures with concerns about exotic viruses entering the U.S. food-chain, or a combination of all the above, the jury is very much still out. But, less well known, is that such events are not limited solely to the United States. The U.K. has been hit hard, too. One particular case stands out for truly memorable and macabre reasons, as will now become apparent. It all began on October 1, 1997, as an extract from one of Nigel Wright's journals reveals:

"Approximately three weeks ago two young men were swimming in Otter Cove [at Lyme Bay, Exmouth, England]. As darkness drew in, they decided to make for the shore and change to go home. As they got changed, one of them looked out to sea. He saw what he described as a 'greenish' light under the surface. He called to the other young man and they both watched as this light 'rose' to the surface of the water. The next thing they knew there was a very bright light shining into their faces. They turned on the scene and fled."

Meanwhile, on the top of the cliffs, equally strange things were afoot. The two young men raced for the car of a relative and breathlessly explained what had happened. Incredibly, she, too, had seen something highly unusual in precisely the same time frame on the road leading to Otter Cove. It was a strange animal that she likened to "an enormous cat." Whatever the origin of the cat-like beast, however, she was certain of one thing: it was, to quote her, "all lit up" – almost glowing, one might say.

On the following day, a dead whale was found washed upon a stretch of beach directly below the cliffs. This did not appear to have been merely a tragic accident, however. On receiving reports that a whale had been found in precisely the area that anomalous lights and a strange creature were seen, Wright quickly launched an investigation.

"The first thing that struck me as I looked on at this scene," recalls Wright, "was how perfect the carcass was. There was no decay or huge chunks torn from it. Then, as I wandered around it, I noticed that there was only one external wound: in the area of the genitals a round incision, the size of a large dinner plate, was cut right into the internal organs of the mammal. The sides of this incision were perfectly formed, as if some giant apple-corer had been inserted and twisted around. From the wound hung some of the internal organs."

Wright continues: "I quizzed the official from English Heritage, who was responsible for the disposal of the carcass. He informed me that no natural predator or boat strike would have caused this wound. As I looked at this sight, the first thing that came into my mind was how this looked just like the cattle mutilation cases of recent times."

Wright was also able to determine that this was not the only time that unusual lights had been seen in the vicinity of Lyme Bay: "No precise date can be given for the evening when a fishing boat encountered a strange light over Lyme Bay," he wrote, "but, since this was told to me by the skipper of the vessel concerned, I can vouch for its authenticity. The vessel in question was five miles off Budleigh Salterton. The crew became aware of a bright white-blue light, which hovered some distance from the boat. At first they thought it was a helicopter but they heard no engine sounds, nor saw any navigation lights."

Wright was told by the captain of the vessel that the night had been "bright and clear" and that if the object had made any noise, it would certainly have been "audible for miles."

"The light remained stationary for about one and a half hours. Judging by the mast of their vessel, which is twenty-eight feet high, the crew estimated that the light was not much higher than that," adds Wright. "It then very suddenly disappeared."

The case was over. Wright's exposure to high-strangeness was not, however.

"They jumped into their car and drove quickly away"

It was also while he was hot on the trail of the Devon events of 1997 that Nigel Wright uncovered a fascinating story concerning the Men in Black. He decided to spend a day looking through the newspaper archives of the Exeter Public Library, in an effort to determine if there had been other waves of paranormal activity in the area, in years long gone. It was while doing so that Wright stumbled on the May 21, 1909 edition of England's *Exmouth Journal* newspaper. Titled *Invasion Scares – Queer Stories from Humberside*, the article reads as follows:

"A strange story was told to the *Yorkshire Post*, Grimsby correspondent by workmen from Killingholm near Immingham new dock works on Tuesday night. They declared that they were seated at noon on the roadside at Killingholm, when a large motor car drove up and two men alighted who walked to the bank on which the workmen were seated and asked if any airships had been recently seen near. The workmen replied: 'No', whereupon the motorists asked the distance between Killingholm and Spurn, and whether any mines were laid in the Humber between the two places. The workmen referred their interrogators to a coastguard, saying he would be able to answer them. It does not matter,' replied the motorists, and, after enquiring the way to the nearest refreshment house, they jumped into their car and drove quickly away."

This is typical behavior of the Men in Black, pulling up in a car, asking questions about unusual aerial vehicles, and driving off again – except for the fact that it's a rarity to find pre-1947 reports of such activity. It may well have been Wright's persistent digging into such matters, and specifically into the matter of the MIB, that led to a dreaded knock on the door. In this case, however, the visitor was a WIW: a Woman in White.

"This thing he is doing with UFOs, tell him to
stop it, right away"

In 2015, Nigel Wright told me: "It was right when we were
in the middle of that huge UFO wave, and I had gone to
an evening meeting of Jon's [Downes] Exeter Strange Phenomena research group. And my wife, Sue, was in the flat
we lived in, in Exmouth. There was a knock at the door. Sue
went to answer it. And when she opened the door, there
stood a lady in all white. It was a lovely, sunny, early evening,
and the woman was dressed in a long, white coat, white
trousers, white headscarf with a little bit of a black fringe
poking through, and huge black sunglasses that wrapped
right around, and very pasty-looking skin. Which was rather
weird, to say the least, with it being hot and sunny.

"Sue said something like, 'Hello can I help you?' And
she asked if I was there. Sue said, 'No, he's out at the moment.
The woman then said, and I'm working from memory now,
of what Sue told me when I got home that night: 'This thing
he is doing with UFOs, tell him to stop it, right away!' Sue
asked why, and this woman didn't say another thing – at all.
She just stared for a moment, then turned and walked down
towards the gate.

"Then something strange happened: the road we lived
on was a long, dead straight road, about 150 to 200 yards
in each direction. As the woman went down the path, Sue
turned to pick up our youngster, who was crying, and when

she turned back again, about ten seconds later, there was no sign of her in either direction. Sue went to the road and looked both ways and there was no one, for as far as Sue could see. She had just vanished.

"It was very odd because just the night before this all happened, I had a hypnotic regression done on a blocked experience from when I was a kid, in which I think I was taken on-board a UFO. And, I actually discussed all this at Jon's meeting – which would have been the same time the woman was visiting the house. That warning to keep off sounds terribly familiar, doesn't it?"

Yes, it most certainly does. It was an event that Nigel Wright still cannot banish from his mind, almost two decades later. Such is the lasting, traumatic effect that these sinister characters have on those whose lives they intrude upon. And, it must be noted, Wright's visitor – or, rather, his wife's visitor – sounds incredibly like Truman Bethurum's 1950s-era Aura Rhanes, and Bruce Lee's mysterious and downright hostile woman that he encountered in a New York bookshop in the winter of 1987. The headscarf and the sunglasses are perfect examples of the camouflaged-based similarities.

We should also note that the visit to the family home followed Nigel Wright's day spent at his local library, and where he came across the 1909 MIB report cited above. We have, you will recall, seen connections between libraries and both the WIB and the MIB on no less than two, previous occasions, and in relation to (A) the 1967 affair of Jane, an acquaintance of radio-host Jaye P. Paro, and also a confidante of John Keel; and (B) the 1980 saga of Peter Rojcewicz at the Library of the University of Pennsylvania.

Do the Women in Black and the Men in Black have a particular liking for books? Maybe so.

"Her eyes make her look evil"

Not only that, there are others who, like Nigel Wright, had abduction experiences earlier in life and who caught the attention of the WIB. One of those was a man named Dan Seldin. A factory worker from Cleveland, Ohio, Seldin, in 1985, contacted the late Budd Hopkins – a noted abduction researcher and the author of *Missing Time* – about an experience which occurred in 1969. It all went down when he, Seldin, was out in nearby Cleveland woods with several friends. Vague memories of a huge object hanging in the sky, a blinding light that lit up the trees, and a vanished period of about an hour of time, were the staple parts of the story. Clearly, something significant occurred, but what?

Two months after contacting Hopkins, Seldin visited him in New York, where hypnosis was used to try and secure yet more data from Seldin's subconscious. It was a session that worked – almost too well. A traumatic story surfaced of Seldin being taken on-board a UFO by a group of small, "frightening-looking" creatures, and then being subjected to distressing medical procedures, including the collection of samples of Seldin's sperm. Other, earlier accounts surfaced, too, suggesting that Seldin was very possibly a lifelong abductee. But particularly fascinating was a "dream" that Seldin had just a couple of months before he and Hopkins met.

As Seldin told the story to Hopkins, he was in bed in the early hours and suddenly found himself wide awake. Standing in the thick shadows, at a distance of around twenty feet, was a trio of large-headed, emotionless humanoids with black eyes and dressed all in black. Then, as if out of nowhere, the face of a human-looking woman loomed into view. It was a chilling sight for Seldin. The malevolent looking she-hag had long, black hair - which swung, or blew, wildly in Seldin's face. In addition, she had dark eyes, and, rather oddly, no teeth.

Seldin was terrified, but he admitted that although the woman gave off an air of "evil," she "looks pretty, too. Her eyes make her look evil. Ugly eyes. They were pretty horrendous eyes, all black and shiny. Blacker than hell."

As Seldin stared upwards at the woman, and frozen to the core with fear, she mounted him and he soon ejaculated. Interestingly, Seldin suspected the black-haired and black-eyed woman was far from pleased with the result – something which, he suggested, may have been because he had had a vasectomy, post-the 1969 encounter, effectively rendering him sterile.

15

"Late at night the attic became a creepy place"

During the early part of 1998, the British Government's House of Commons held a fascinating and arguably near-unique debate on the existence – or otherwise – of a particular breed of mysterious animal that is widely rumored, and even accepted by many, to inhabit the confines of the United Kingdom: the so-called Alien Big Cats, or ABCs, as they have become infamously known. It scarcely needs mentioning that the U.K. is not home to an indigenous species of large cat. Nevertheless, for decades amazing stories have circulated from all across the nation of sightings of large, predatory cats that savagely feed on both livestock and wild animals and that terrify, intrigue and amaze the local populace in the process. And, of course, the media loves them, one and all.

As history has demonstrated, there now exists a very large and credible body of data in support of the notion that the U.K. does have within its midst a healthy and thriving population of presently unidentified large cats – such as the

infamous Beast of Bodmin and the Beast of Exmoor that
so hysterically dominated the nation's newspapers and TV
news back in the early-to-mid 1980s. But never mind just
the 1980s – reports continue to thrive to this very day.

There is, however, an aspect of the ABC mystery that
doesn't always get the coverage it should: the strange connection to the mysterious Women in Black and "government
officials" that, allegedly, at least, are intent on keeping any
and all hard evidence of the existence of the beasts under
wraps and out of the hands of the public and the media.

It might seem strange that there could be a cover-up of
the ABC phenomenon in the U.K., when the media is practically reporting on them – somewhere in the land – at least
a couple of times per week. But, there's a vast chasm between
(A) the press titillating and exciting their readers with tales
of large, predatory cats on the loose and (B) actually pre-
senting hard evidence of such creatures in the nation's midst.
The stories of the big cats of the U.K. undeniably entertain
and intrigue the British public. That, however, is very different to – hypothetically – someone finding a dead mountain
lion by the side of the road and the story then becoming a
stark and serious one of potential man-eating proportions.

Clearly, we don't see evidence of sinister, black-garbed
women popping up, and silencing witnesses, every time an
ABC is seen in the U.K. But, they have surfaced on more
than a few occasions, and particularly so when claims are
made about ABC corpses being found or seen (by the side

of a country road, for instance). Merrily Harpur's book, *Mystery Big Cats*, includes a number of cases that suggest the British Government's DEFRA – the Department for Environment, Food and Rural Affairs – may have played a role in confiscating the evidence that large, unknown cats really are prowling around the landscape of the United Kingdom. Other reports, however, have distinct paranormal overtones to them – and many of them come from a 26-square-mile area of woodland and heathland in central England called the Cannock Chase. As you will now see.

"No-one will ever tell me there isn't something funny about black-panthers in England"

Eileen Allen says that she caught sight of a "big black panther," as she described it, while she was visiting the Cannock Chase woods in the latter part of 1996. The overwhelming shock of seeing the immense beast lurking near one of the head-stones in a local cemetery, and staring intently in Allen's direction, was nothing compared to the absolute terror that struck her when the creature suddenly vanished – and I do mean literally vanished. We're talking about into thin-air - amid a sound that Allen described as "like an electricity cracking noise." Unsurprisingly, Allen did not hang around and quickly left the cemetery. To this very day, she has never returned; nor does she have any plans to do so in the future, either. Who can blame her for that? She also believes that a series of anonymous, hang-up phone calls she received in the early hours - and which begun the very night after her encounter occurred, and which continued for several days - were somehow connected to her sighting.

Bob Parker experienced something very similar in the woods barely a quarter of a mile or so from the cemetery in late 2000, while walking his dog on one particular Sunday morning. In this case, a large black cat came hurtling violently through the heather, skidded onto the pathway that Parker was following, and bounded off, apparently not at all bothered or concerned by the presence of either Parker or his little Corgi dog, Paddy. Seeing a big cat was astounding enough in itself; but what happened next was just downright bizarre.

Parker says that: "Me and the dog just froze solid. I couldn't believe it; could *not* believe it. But when [the cat] got about fifty feet from us, it literally sort of dived at the ground. It sort of took a leap up and almost dive-bombed the path, and went right through and vanished, just like that. I know exactly how it sounds, so don't tell me. But that's exactly what happened: it was like it just melted into the path."

Equally as strange, but for very different reasons, is the story of Sally Ward. She claims that back in the late-1960s, while she and her husband were walking across the Cannock Chase, not too far from the green and pleasant Milford Common, on what was a wintry and very foggy morning, they almost literally stumbled upon what she described as "a black panther; a real one" that was sitting "bolt-upright" on an open stretch of ground to their left, and approximately thirty feet from them. But that was not the strangest spectacle, however. Also stood upright around the huge beast was what Ward described as: "…seven or eight other cats. But normal cats: pet cats."

She was sure that the smaller animals were not "big-cat kittens," but were "the sort of cats anyone would own. I don't know anything about panthers and lions and tigers, but I know a normal cat when I see one." Rather strangely, all of the smaller cats were staring, in almost hypnotic fashion and in complete silence, at the large black cat, as if utterly transfixed by its proud stance and powerful, muscular presence.

The Ward's, perhaps quite naturally, felt very ill at ease with the whole surreal and eerie situation, and both slowly and cautiously continued past the group, and then raced down to their car, which they had parked in Milford. Ward's husband was, at first at least, fully intent on reporting the encounter to the local police; but after Mrs. Ward pleaded otherwise, they decided to remain silent – aside from quietly confiding in various friends over the years and decades. To this day, Sally Ward stands by her story with total, firm conviction: "No-one will ever tell me there isn't something funny about black-panthers in England."

Given that, as the above cases demonstrate, there is a clear and undeniable paranormal component to the ABC enigma, let's take a look at the connection between the Alien Big Cats and the Women in Black.

Beware of the cat! (U.S. Fish & Wildlife Service, 2002).

An underground encounter and a visit from a WIB

We will begin with the story of Maureen Abbott. She saw, when she was in her twenties, what she describes as a large "black panther" [in reality, "black panthers" are simply melanistic big-cats, such as cougars and leopards, whose bodies contain an over-abundance of dark pigmentation], late one winter evening in either 1954 or 1955. Astonishingly, it was doing nothing less than racing along the track as she stood, alone, awaiting a train on the Bakerloo Line of the London, England underground rail-system. That Abbott found herself utterly alone – and with not a single other passenger, or rail employee, in sight - provoked a very weird and unsettling feeling that Abbott was unable to fully describe. "A bit like a dream" was her concise explanation.

Describing the animal as running very fast, she said that as it passed her, it quickly looked in her direction, with a menace-filled frown on its visage, before vanishing into the darkness of the tunnels. Although Abbott did not see the creature again, she has never forgotten her brief, terrifying encounter with the unknown, deep below the city of London. There is a *very* curious sequel to Abbott's encounter: two-days later, she was visited at her home by a woman in black who flashed government credentials and who, while the pair sat and drank cups of tea, advised Abbott, in fairly relaxed tones, not to talk about the experience. To this day, Abbott still recalls how uneasy she felt in the presence of what was an extremely pale-faced, near-emotionless WIB who left Abbott feeling as if, "…I had to vacuum the house after she left."

Phone calls and dead cats

Aside from visits by WIB types and the confiscation of corpses, there is another angle to the ABC puzzle: that of telephone interference. On many occasions, witnesses to UFOs have received strange and unsettling phone calls in the wake of their encounters. Odd, slightly foreign sounding, female voices warn people not to talk about their encounters. Weird and unsettling electronic bleeps and screeches, and unintelligible rapid chatter are commonplace. And that applies to the ABC issue too. I can't say that my records are bulging on this angle, as they certainly are not. But I do have seven reports on file where witnesses were on the receiving end of what can only be described as telephone harassment – and specifically by unknown women.

Notably, in two of those seven cases, the witnesses claimed to have seen the bodies of dead ABCs: one was seen by the side of a road near the English village of Blakeney in 1986, by a shift-worker on his way home, around 3:00 a.m. The other body was almost literally stumbled upon, in October 1987, in an area of woodland near the English town of Bradford-on- Avon, during the early afternoon. In both cases, the cats were very large, powerful-looking, and completely black in color. Neither witness told anyone – outside of their immediate family – anything about their encounters, chiefly because they had nothing to back up the claims.

In the first case, the witness returned to the site at daybreak, at roughly 7:30 a.m., and the body was gone. In the second case, precisely the same thing happened: when the frightened witness told her husband what she had seen, he accompanied her back to the site, around three or four hours later, after he returned home from work. That body, too, had curiously vanished. In both instances, however

– and despite neither party having made an official report or having informed the local press – the witnesses were on the near-immediate receiving end of odd phone calls, filled with what can only be described as classic WIB-type interference and intimidation. In both cases, there were undercurrents of menace from the WIB, the thrust of the calls clearly being to encourage the witnesses not to talk about what they had seen – namely, the apparent dead remains of ABCs.

So, what's going on? Do certain elements of the British Government know – with absolute certainty – that the ABCs are 100 percent real? And, if so, are they doing their very best to prevent what is seen as an entertaining mystery by most, from mutating into something that could provoke widespread concern, and perhaps even hysteria, among the population? Or, do the undeniable WIB-like overtones to such cases suggest the ABCs are less than flesh-and-blood and far more paranormal-themed? Maybe the truth lies in a combination of both realms. Someone, deep within the heart of officialdom, may very well know something that they don't want the rest of us to know. Or, perhaps, that same "someone" may be from a far darker, supernatural domain. That is made all the more likely by the fact that none other than Brian Kinnersley, a central figure in the saga of Sir Peter Horsley's Woman in Black, encountered an Alien Big Cat in the countryside of Staffordshire, England in 2002.

Back to Albert Bender

One final thing: it may not be entirely coincidental that none other than Albert Bender had an absolute obsession with anomalous black cats. As we saw earlier, in the late 1940s, Bender decided to turn his attic-based bedroom/living-room into what he himself termed his very own "Chamber of Horrors." Bender decorated the room with ghoulish imagery of monsters, vampires, werewolves, and skeletons.

On top of that, practically one entire wall of the bedroom was adorned with paintings and cut-outs of large, black cats – some in prowling fashion and others standing to attention; their wild, staring eyes near-hypnotizing those that dared to look at them. One has to wonder if Bender – whose family had a chilling WIB in their midst, as far back as the early 1930s, as was noted in Chapter One of this book – knew something of the WIB-Alien Big Cat phenomenon. If he did, then perhaps, as a result, he chose to present his knowledge, in cryptic fashion, on the walls of his Chamber of Horrors.

In Bender's own words:

"Late at night the attic became a creepy place. The floor boards creaked as you walked upon them, and on dark windy evenings stranger noises came from it. Visitors were often 'shaken up' and uncomfortable, as I laughed heartily at their nervousness and amused myself by relating ghost stories at times. My friends eventually decided they enjoyed the spooky atmosphere and that probably was another reason for my fixing up the 'chamber of horrors' by painting grotesque scenes and faces upon the walls of the room. After about eight months I had done so good a job that it almost frightened me when I stood back and looked at all of it one evening. No wonder my friends found it so fascinating, for so many of the ghostly characters appeared to be looking straight at me, no matter where I might be in the room."

Researcher Riley Crabb noted that Bender "added to the spooky atmosphere by adding a collection of twenty chiming clocks, which banged away at the quarter, the half and the hour. One wall of the room was still empty. To this he added a full color painting of the solar system and, of all things, a sketch of his conception of the hidden side of the moon, which caused much comment and conjecture."

As we have seen, and just like Albert Bender, the MIB are obsessed by time.

Crabb also noted, very significantly, that Bender said: "Developing my horror motif further, I discarded my table ornaments and substituted macabre items such as artificial human skulls, shrunken heads, bats, spiders, snakes, *black panthers* and the like.'"

Did Albert Bender know something of the WIB/MIB/ABC connection? Is this the reason why almost one entire wall of his "chamber of horrors" was filled with images of what can only be described as Alien Big Cats? The question remains, and is likely remain, as intriguing as it is unresolved.

16

"May I come in?"

Colin Perks - an Englishman who died prematurely in 2009 - was for years possessed by a definitive obsession. As a child, Perks became fascinated by the legends pertaining to one of the most well-known and cherished figures of British folklore: King Arthur. For Perks, however, Arthur was far more than mere myth. Perks, like so many other students of Arthurian lore, came to believe that the stories of King Arthur were based upon the exploits and battles of an all too real ruler of that name. This Arthur held sway over significant portions of ancient Britain from the latter part of the 5th Century to the early part of the 6th. He and his fearless soldiers bravely fought off invading hordes of Germanic Saxons and, as a result, left major marks upon British history and mythology.

By the time Perks reached his thirties, he was the proud possessor of a huge library on all-things of a King Arthur-themed nature. His research, by now, was not just focused on the past, however. Rather, Perks, following clues that he believed were hidden in a series of complex codes and ciphers that had been provided to him by a fellow Arthur-enthusiast in 1978, was a man on a mission to find the final resting place of King Arthur. The location, Perks concluded, was somewhere in the vicinity of the old English town of Glastonbury.

Glastonbury Abbey, a favorite haunt of doomed Colin Perks (Nick Redfern, 2000).

With origins that date back thousands of years - to the Neolithic era, no less – Glastonbury is noted for its atmospheric, centuries-old abbey, its links to the story of the Holy Grail (the cup alleged to have held the blood of Christ), and even claims that Jesus himself once visited the town. Today, Glastonbury is a hotbed of new-age stores, bookshops, meditation centers, and haunted old inns and hotels. The town is enveloped by a captivating and almost magical atmosphere. It echoes back to a time long gone, but one which still tenaciously clings to life in this little town, and where the mysterious traditions of old still stand solid. For many years, Colin Perks dwelled in Glastonbury, tirelessly searching for the underground vault that he believed existed nearby and which housed the remains of King Arthur. And, perhaps, still houses those remains.

As the 20th century neared its end, Perks' research to try and find Arthur's grave reached its height. He was, by now, convinced that the location was somewhere within a small area of woodland situated just a few miles from Glastonbury itself. When time allowed, Perks headed off into the heart of the woods, metal-detector and shovel in hand, trying to uncover evidence that deep below the enchanting woodland floor lay the remains of one of Britain's mightiest warrior-kings.

A stranger in the night
- -

Late one evening in September 2000, and after a day and evening spent digging in the woods, Perks received a strange, and somewhat disturbing, phone call. It was from a woman who made it very clear that she wanted to discuss with Perks his studies of an Arthurian nature. She also made it clear she would not take "no" for an answer.

Colin Perks found this highly worrying, since his phone number was not listed in the telephone directory. On top of that, he had no family, aside from a very elderly mother in a nursing-home, and he rarely discussed his research with anyone. Nevertheless, the mysterious woman at the other end of the line clearly knew all about him, even including his forays into the old, nearby woods in search of King Arthur's remains. Perks was puzzled, disturbed, and intrigued by the call. As a result, he agreed to a face-to-face meeting. It was a decision he sorely came to regret.

Several nights later, and at the arranged time of 7:00 p.m., there was a knock at the door. Perks took a deep breath and opened it. He was confronted by what can only be described as a Woman in Black. Standing before him was a beautiful woman, thirty-five to forty years of age. She was dressed in a smart and expensive-looking outfit, had a long and full-bodied head of black hair, and just about the palest and smoothest skin possible. For a moment there was silence. Perks simply stared, feeling various parts captivated, intimidated, and downright frightened. Although the woman's face appeared utterly emotionless, Perks detected a hard to define air of hostility, and perhaps even hatred, of him. This was hardly a good start to the evening. And it proceeded to get even worse.

The silence and eerie awkwardness was only broken when, after about twenty seconds, the woman said: "My name is Sarah Key. May I come in?" Perks nodded and the woman entered his abode, made her way straight to his couch, sat down, and motioned him to follow by patting the cushion next to her. It was immediately clear who was running the show. And it was not unlike the situation that Sir Peter Horsley found himself when faced with the mysterious Mrs. Markham back in the 1950s. The strange atmosphere was only amplified by the howling wind and the driving rain that battered the windows of Perks' apartment. It was then that Perks realized Sarah Key's skin, hair, and outfit were all totally dry. How she was able to remain free of the pummeling deluge, without the benefit of an umbrella, was a mystery, indeed.

Spied on and followed

Wasting no time, Sarah Key got straight to the point and informed Perks that she, and what she described as her "colleagues," had been carefully watching him for years. She added, in no uncertain terms, that the purpose of her visit was to request that Perks cease his research. As in, right now. A suddenly defensive Perks loudly responded that there was no way he would ever stop his work to find King Arthur's burial site. On top of that he scoffed at the very idea that shadowy figures were watching his every move, both in Glastonbury and in the heart of the old woods. Or, it's more correct to say he scoffed until Sarah Keey reeled off fact upon fact about where Perks was on specific days and nights, even down to which local pubs he visited for dinner and a pint of Guinness after his nightly work of toiling in the woods was over. That's when the scoffing came to a shuddering halt.

As Colin Perks sat silently, Sarah Key continued that Arthur's grave – or his "chamber," as she specifically described it - was no ordinary resting place. Rather, it was built atop a paranormal gateway, a portal to other dimensions where there dwelled hideous and terrible beasts of the kind that would have made H.P. Lovecraft forever pleased and proud. The chamber had been constructed as a means to prevent the foul things of this strange realm from entering our world. Perks' dabbling and digging, Key told him, might have been innocent and earnest, but he was playing with definitive fire of a type that could provoke catastrophe and carnage if the magical "gateway" was opened.

Sarah Key's tone then became undeniably threatening and her face became grim in the extreme. She explained that if Perks did not give up his quest, he would receive yet another visit. From who, or what, was not made entirely clear, but Perks knew it was destined to be nothing positive or friendly. At that point, Key stood up and, rather inexplicably, picked up from the living-room table a pen of Perks' and placed it into one of the pockets of her jacket. She laughed slyly as she did so, to the extent that a chilled-to-the-bone Perks dared not ask for it back. Notably, in centuries past the "wee folk," such as fairies and goblins, invariably stole innocuous items when they visited the world of humans, and which they took back with them to their own strange realms of existence - as an odd kind of memento. And, recall, back in the 1960s a MIB stole the pen of one of John Keel's closest friends, Mary Hyre – an investigator of the Mothman enigma, which descended on Point Pleasant, West Virginia in the mid-1960s.

Sarah Key repeated her words of warning at the door and suggested, in the strongest tones, that Perks give up his obsession. Or else. Perks did not, however. As a result, the second visitor that Sarah Key warned about soon turned up.

A winged monster pays a terrifying visit

It was roughly two months later, and late at night, when Perks had a truly terrifying encounter. He was driving back to Glastonbury from the city of Bath – which, like Glastonbury, is also located in the English county of Somerset. On one piece of road that lacked illumination, and which was curiously free of any other traffic, a bizarre figure suddenly materialized in the road ahead. Luckily, as the road was a small and winding one, Perks' speed was barely twenty-five miles per hour, which gave him time to quickly slam on the brakes. In front of him was what can only be described as the closest thing one could imagine to a gargoyle. That's to say a tall, man-like figure sporting nothing less than a large pair of bat-style wings. A pair of blazing red eyes penetrated Perks' very soul. Hysterical with fear, Perks hit the accelerator pedal and the creature vanished in front of his eyes, and just before impact could occur. Matters weren't quite over, however.

One week later, and not long after the witching-hour, Perks was awakened from his sleep by the horrific sight of the gargoyle looming menacingly over his bed. Paralyzed with fear, and with the creature gripping his wrists tightly, Perks could only stare in utter shock as the beast delivered a telepathic-style message to stay away from the woods, and to cease looking for the chamber of King Arthur. An instant later, the monstrous form was gone. Perks wondered for a few seconds if it had all been a horrific nightmare. In his heart of hearts, however, he knew it wasn't. In fact, Perks ultimately came to believe that Sarah Key – Perks' very own Woman in Black – and the gargoyle were not just inter-connected. Rather, he concluded that they were one and the same. For Perks, Key was a hideous and supernatural shape-shifter, one that could take on any form it desired, including that of something akin to a gargoyle. And a beautiful Woman in Black, too, of course.

This did not, however, deter Perks from continuing his research. He continued for the next eight years, never ulti-mately finding the resting place of King Arthur, whether in those mysterious woods or elsewhere. Nor did he receive a follow-up visit of the WIB kind. That was not the end of the high-strangeness, however. In 2002, Perks claimed to have photographed, from his position on a bridge, nothing less than a sea serpent traversing the waters of London's famous River Thames – and in an area of the river that was directly opposite the headquarters of MI6, which is the British equivalent of the CIA. Precisely what all this meant, Perks never knew, but he felt that the sighting of the alleged creature, and its close proximity to MI6 was intended as a warning to keep away from things that didn't concern him. Such was Perks' concern about the photograph, he mailed it to me, forever wishing to wash his hands of it. I said to Perks, when I received the picture, that to me it looked like a thin log bobbing along on the water. Perks replied that even if that was the case, the fact that it appeared to resemble a serpent – and that he was there at the very time it appeared, and with his camera, no less – was evidence of some kind of supernatural, "trickster"-style phenomenon giving him a warning.

A monster of the River Thames? Or just a log?
(Colin Perks, 2002).

If it was such a warning, it's somewhat unsettling – and undeniably tragic – that death came for Perks while he was only in his sixties. Whether Colin Perks' death was due to bad luck, ill-health, or the actions of Sarah Key – perhaps the ultimate British Woman in Black – is something we will likely never know. The mystery of King Arthur – and of that alluring, menacing and dark-garbed beauty – remains.

When matters get "even more serious"

There is a very interesting, and *extremely* similar, parallel to the ultimately tragic affair of Colin Perks. It adds a great deal of weight to Perks' claim that someone was trying to silence those who just might be getting too close to the truth surrounding certain characters from British folklore, legend, and mythology.

The story revolves around a man named Michael "Drew" Hartley, a freelance television producer from Brighouse, West Yorkshire, England. In 1996, Hartley came up with the idea of putting a show together on a certain monument near the English village of Clifton. It marks the alleged grave of none other than yet another fabled, English hero: Robin Hood. Both Kirklees Priory – a 12th century structure – and Kirklees Hall, which was built in the 16th century, play a role in the story. As for the monument, it's a centuries-old structure situated on the Kirklees Estate, the accompanying inscription of which maintains that Robin Hood died on Christmas Eve, in the year 1247, and that his remains are housed within.

In an effort to get the project moving, Hartley brought on board a pair of students from Dewsbury College, as well as an employee of Brighouse Library. They didn't last long, however: in a situation closely mirroring that of Colin Perks in 2000, the two students claimed to have received late night visits from someone who warned them not to have anything, at all, to do with the Robin Hood production. Unless, that is, they wanted to see their futures ruined and their lives plunged into "even more serious" situations. As for the librarian, she suddenly cut off all contact with Hartley, citing other commitments. She wouldn't even speak to him; instead, choosing to sever her ties via a solitary fax.

Notably, at the height of this *very* odd affair, Hartley himself received a phone call from a man with an upper-class English accent, who claimed to be in the employ of MI6, and who, although, not threatening, reeled off a wealth of personal data on Hartley – making it clear to Hartley that he knew all about him. Note that it was on a stretch of the River Thames, London that was overlooked by the MI6 headquarters where Colin Perks claimed to have seen, and photographed, a sea serpent in 2002.

As for Hartley's film on Robin Hood, it was never made.

17

"It was a hideous-looking woman dressed in black"

It's a story that sounds like the kind of thing one would read in the pages of a story by horror maestro H.P. Lovecraft. Except for one key issue: it is one hundred percent fact. It was in the early hours of Friday, January 16, 2004, that a Mexican police officer was attacked by a monstrous, flying, hag-like creature in Guadalupe. All was normal until around 3:00 a.m. That was when all hell broke loose.

Officer Leonardo Samaniego was on his routine patrol in the Colonia Valles de la Salla area when something truly nightmarish occurred. A black figure leapt out of the shadows of a big tree that stood by the side of the road and slowly turned towards the officer's cruiser. This was nothing as down to earth as a large owl, however. Given the time and the darkness, Samaniego put his lights on high beam and directed the car at the thing in the road. The enormity of the situation – and the horrific nature of it – suddenly became all too clear. It was a hideous-looking woman dressed in black. And she was *floating* above the ground.

For a few moments, Officer Samaniego could do nothing but stare in absolute terror as the dark-skinned woman's lidless, black eyes glared directly at him. For a moment. Suddenly, the winged fiend pulled her cloak around her eyes, seemingly affected by the bright light. She then flew at the vehicle, jumped onto the hood and tried to smash her way into the car, via the windshield and with her bony-but-powerful clenched fists. Panicked Samaniego managed to put his car in reverse and he hit the accelerator. As the vehicle shot away at a quick rate, the monster-woman clung onto the windshield, still intent on getting inside the car. Suddenly, the car slammed into a wall and came to a – quite literally – crashing halt.

For a few moments, Samaniego covered his eyes. But it was to no avail: when he moved his hands away the hag was still there, on the hood, and staring malevolently at him. Such was the level of his fear, he actually fainted at the wheel. In minutes paramedics were on the scene. The beast had gone, and Samaniego fortunately soon recovered. Rather incredibly, it turned out that when Samaniego told his story to his superior officers, it prompted others in the department to admit that they, too, had seen the flying witch-woman in the dead of night, but had failed to report their encounters for fear of ridicule.

In May 2009, a San Antonio, Texas-based cryptozoologist and friend, Ken Gerhard, traveled to Mexico and had the very good fortune to interview Officer Samaniego firsthand, along with a television crew from the History Channel's popular show, *Monster Quest.* Gerhard recalls how traumatic the whole affair was for Samaniego, even five years after it had occurred:

"At several junctures he began to become emotional and tear up as he relived that terrifying evening that had changed his life forever. Leonardo confessed to us that he still had vivid nightmares about the encounter and occasionally woke up in a panic with sweat streaming down his face. I wondered if the fact that I was dressed all in black with my trademark black leather cowboy hat (adorned with a silver skull, no less) made him slightly uncomfortable."

Monster-hunter, Ken Gerhard. (Nick Redfern, 2014).

While in Guadalupe, Gerhard had the good fortune to meet with someone else who had had a similar, traumatic experience when he was a young boy. His name is Marco Reynoso, a UFO investigator and the former head of the regional office of the U.S.-based Mutual UFO Network. Back to Gerhard:

"Over breakfast, he told me about a remarkable experience that had set him on a lifelong quest for real answers. Apparently, when he was a young boy growing up in Monterrey, Marco had observed a tiny, winged, humanoid-like creature peeking out from behind his kitchen curtains one evening. The diminutive being reminded him of a gargoyle, with long, black hair covering its body and bat-like wings. To his credit, Marco made an attempt to curtail the goblin, but the entity vanished right before his eyes."

Ken Gerhard has uncovered other reports of flying humanoids in Mexico, some with wings and others that appear to have the ability to float in the sky and without the need for wings. He has also collected a great deal of reports of what sound astonishingly like presumed extinct pterosaurs from the Jurassic era. Clearly, something strange is afoot in the skies of Mexico. And particularly so after sunset.

The WIB, the MIB, and a Monster

For years, sensational and sinister stories have surfaced from the forests and lowlands of Puerto Rico that tell of a strange and lethal creature roaming the landscape by night and day, while striking overwhelming terror into the hearts of the populace. This is not at all surprising since the animal has been described as having a pair of glowing red eyes, powerful, claw style hands, razor sharp teeth, a body not unlike that a monkey, a row of vicious spikes running down the length of its back, and occasionally, and of deep relevance to this particular chapter, a pair of large and leathery bat-like wings.

And if that is not enough: the beast is said to feed on the blood of the local animal - and predominantly goat – population, after puncturing their jugular veins with two sharp teeth. That's correct: Puerto Rico has a monstrous vampire in its midst. Its name is the Chupacabra, a Spanish term, very appropriately meaning Goat-Sucker.

Theories abound with respect to the nature of the beast, with some researchers and witnesses suggesting that the monster is some form of giant-bat; others prefer the theory that it has extraterrestrial origins; while the most bizarre idea postulated is that the Chupacabras is the creation of a top secret, genetic research laboratory hidden deep within Puerto Rico's El Yunque rainforest, which is located in the Sierra de Luquillo, approximately forty kilometers southeast of the city of San Juan.

On a number of occasions, I have traveled to the island of Puerto Rico to try and seek out the vampire-like Chupacabra for myself, and, perhaps one day, even to determine its true nature. On one particular occasion, while roaming around Puerto Rico in 2005 with Canadian filmmaker Paul Kimball (we were there to make a documentary titled *Fields of Fear*), I had the very good fortune to meet and interview a man named Antonio, a pig-farmer who had an unusual experience in 2000 that led to a decidedly strange visit from a Woman in Black/Man in Black duo.

As Antonio told me, one of his animals had been killed, after darkness had fallen, by the now familiar puncture marks to the neck. In this case, however, the animal exhibited three such marks, rather than the usual two. In addition, a number of rabbits kept on the property had been slaughtered in identical fashion.

At the time that all of the carnage was taking place, a considerable commotion was, quite naturally, being made by the rest of Antonio's animals. As a result, upon hearing this, he rushed wildly out of his house with a machete in his hand, and flung it hard in the direction of the marauding predator. Very strangely, he told me, the makeshift weapon seemed to bounce off something that seemed distinctly metallic in nature.

In fact, Antonio suggested that what the machete had made contact with seemed armor-plated in nature. Due to the overwhelming darkness, however, he had no idea what the creature may have been. But something deadly was most certainly prowling around the property. The machete was later given to Antonio's cousin for safekeeping. The most confounding aspect of the affair was still to come, however. That's right: Antonio was about to get a visit of the type we have encountered time and again in these pages.

Shortly after the killing of the pig and the rabbits, a man and woman – dressed in typical, official-looking black regalia, on a stifling hot day, no less, and who announced they worked for NASA – arrived at the farm and quickly proceeded to ask Antonio a wealth of questions about what had occurred, what he had seen, and the way in which his animals had met their grisly fates.

When the conversation was over, the pair thanked the bemused farmer, in a fashion befitting both the Women in Black and the Men in Black – wholly unemotionally, in other words - and left without uttering another, single word. How the dark duo even knew that the attacks had taken place, and why on earth NASA would be dispatching personnel to his farm to investigate them, Antonio had no idea at all.

One thing that Antonio told me he had held back from informing his two mysterious visitors was that on the morning after the attack he had found strange footprints on his property that were spread quite a distance from each other; and he formed the opinion that whatever had made them, had the ability to leap considerable distances, in a fashion similar to that of a Kangaroo – or, perhaps even, he mused, it had the ability to fly.

Leaping or flying monsters, Men and Women in Black, and mutilated animals collectively suggested that something highly strange was, and perhaps still is, afoot on Puerto Rico.

<u>18</u>

"I used to apprentice as an embalmer, and I swear that woman smelled just like formalin"

The following account, sent to me by a Facebook friend, is without doubt one of the most disturbing and chilling stories of the WIB kind that I have on record. Titled "Possible WIB and MIB Encounter in Florida," it begins as follows and relates events which occurred in late 2008:

"Dear Mr. Redfern, I have an interest in Forteana and 'high-strangeness,' but I've always been a skeptic and only researched the subjects from a folklorist's point of view. However, I have had one experience that a friend of mine said I should send to you, so here it is. I was speaking at the IAFA (International Association of Fantasy in the Arts) conference this March and attended a speech of a friend who spoke on high-strangeness in the desert and MIB. I told her of my experience, and she said, 'You NEED to tell this to Nick Redfern!' I had read some of your blog posts about the nature of Bigfoot-type entities (I agree with you there is more to them than an unknown ape, but I won't digress) and knew you had written books on the subject of MIB.

"I worked as a bar manager at a sports bar in Tampa, Florida, and at 2:00 AM I cashed out the servers and sent them home and closed down the kitchen. The bar itself closed at 3:00 AM, but my last few barflies stumbled out before 2:30. I closed out the credit cards, counted the register, turned off the jukebox, and sat down to wait out the clock. At about ten minutes to three a couple walked in. I told them it was last call and cash only at this point, and locked the doors behind them, not even really paying attention to them (rude, I know, but after 12 hours, give me a break). When I did notice them, I began to feel uneasy."

"She had the same high forehead, cheekbones, and blue eyes as her partner"

"Neither one of them sat down on the stools in front of the bar. They each ordered a non-alcoholic beer, and then just stood there holding their drinks, about two stools apart. Then I noticed how they were dressed. I dress in a 'goth' style and prefer black, but these two were definitely not goths, despite the (almost) all-black attire. The man, who appeared older than the woman, maybe about 40-ish, wore a black double-breasted suit of an outdated cut. I'd say maybe 1950's style, with a rumpled black shirt and a crooked black tie.

"I'd say he was about 5'9 with a thin build. He had

incredibly pale skin that showed blue veins underneath (I had turned on all of the house lights by this point, so they stood out in stark contrast), a very high forehead, prominent cheekbones, and deep-set, large, brilliant blue eyes, possibly the most vibrant blue I have ever seen. He had thin, dry, unhealthy-looking silvery-grey hair pulled back in a pony-tail, with seemingly random dark brown patches in it, as if he gave a half-assed attempt to dye it and gave up halfway through the process.

"The woman, who was about 5'6, emaciated, and looked about mid-20s, wore a black evening gown with elbow-length satin gloves and had a clashing bright green knit shawl around her shoulders. She had a short bob haircut with bangs, though it really looked like a poorly cared-for wig. She had the same high forehead, cheekbones, and blue eyes as her partner, although her eyes were narrower and slightly slanted. Neither one had eyebrows. As I started cleaning up behind the bar, the woman began clearing her throat impatiently, so I walked over to see what they wanted (I wanted them to get the hell out of my bar.) That's when I noticed the stench emanating from this woman. Not only did she smell like she hadn't bathed in a month, she also smelled like chemicals. I used to apprentice as an embalmer, and I swear that woman smelled just like formalin."

"Even though the man was talking, she was the
one in charge"

"When I walked over, the man beckoned me to him and
placed a black leather satchel on the bar, from which he
removed several photographs and asked me if I knew any of
the subjects in those pictures. I decided I would humor him
(part of me suspected this must be a police investigation),
but when I looked at the pictures I became truly terrified.
As I said, I am in the Goth culture here in Tampa, and as I
am sure you know, that subculture attracts many paranormal
enthusiasts, Wiccans, Satanists, occultists, and so on. Some
of the people in these photographs were my friends! Most
of the photos looked candid and snapped from hiding, and
some of them bore time stamps and were obviously stills
from CCTV footage.

"As I looked over the photos, the Stinky Bitch (pardon
the term, but it fits!) kept staring and grinning at me. I had
the feeling that even though the man was talking, she was
the one in charge. I have no idea why I knew this, but I did.
I feigned ignorance and told them I had no idea who those
people were, and that I was closing now, so they needed
to leave. Mind you, they never sat down during this entire
period. They both grinned at me like they knew I was lying,
the man unlocked the door, and both quietly walked out.
They had not even taken a sip from their beers.

"The whole experience seemed dream-like to me, and I

almost wanted to believe I had hallucinated it. Remember how I said I abused my free credits on the jukebox? Well, once the two left I realized the juke was dead. I even remember what bands were playing before the two walked in: Iron Maiden followed by Siouxsie and the Banshees. That particular model of jukebox cannot be shut off by the remote; it would only die like that in the event of a power outage or if it had been unplugged. It was still plugged in, and no power outage had occurred. The bar closed two months later and I never saw the two again. There is my event, and you are the third person I have shared this with, after my friend and my wife. I would like to remain anonymous if you choose to use this in your future work, as in addition to a wife I have a step-daughter. Feel free to contact me if you have any further questions. - A Hesitant Believer."

After reading "AHB's" account, I quickly wrote back, and got the following reply:

"Someone kept calling the bar on my nights off,
asking for me by my full name"

"Mr. Redfern, My experience happened in late November of 2008. The bar in which I worked was in a strip mall, and all of the other businesses had closed long before midnight, with the exception of the American faux-Irish pub on the other side of the complex, which that night got shut down by police shortly after 1:00 AM (I don't think this was any part of a conspiracy, since that place got busted at least every couple of weeks). I told you I had sent the servers home, and as far as I know, I was completely alone in that strip mall when my visitors arrived.

"After I received your reply I contacted my former assistant manager and the one server I still keep in contact with, and asked them, nonchalantly, if they had experienced any odd occurrences involving black cars or odd phone calls. I did not tell them why I was asking. Neither I, nor they, had any experiences with black cars, but they both told me that someone kept calling the bar on my nights off, asking for me by my full name. These calls only occurred in the two weeks prior to my encounter (or whatever you want to call it). No one outside of my family, close friends and lawyer know my middle name. It's not even on my social security card.

"Both the assistant manager and server told me that after they said I was not working that night, the voice on the other end, always female, would giggle and hang up. This really scared me after what you said about strange phone calls (as I said, I am new to actually investigating odd happenings). I spent my day reading your posts about MIB/WIB on Mysterious Universe, and one of your most recent articles startled me. You talked about the 'gypsy women' in New York, and as I read I got goosebumps. Remember how I said the woman wore a clashing bright green shawl?

"At the time I saw those people in my bar I thought, 'Oh, she's a Gypsy,' even though she was corpse pale. That really shocked me, Mr. Redfern. When you said you had many cases that are similar to mine, I did not know whether to feel relieved or terrified. I feel somewhat comforted that I am not delusional and that others have shared these experiences, but am scared that they seem to be so common. And I have a question for you: In your studies have you ever come across individuals that came down with severe illness after encountering these 'people?' Only three days after I saw them I developed a severe bacterial infection on my legs and lower abdomen. It was a Strep infection, and the doctor could not determine how I contracted it. Thank you for listening."

Hardly surprisingly, I did yet another follow-up with "AHB" and received this:

"The more uncomfortable I became, the stranger they acted"

"Thank you for listening to me and taking my experience seriously. To be honest, I had hoped you could debunk that encounter somehow, like attributing it to pranksters, police officials with a sick sense of humor, or my own mind playing tricks on me. I am a stickler when it comes to asking for ID when I tend bar; I would probably card you if you walked in, but I do not remember carding the 'woman,' who I described as being in her twenties. I don't even recall accepting money from the figures for their drinks. I laughed aloud when I read the article that theorized that some MIB encounters may be people with autism, as I myself am autistic (though I have never worn a furry hat).

"I am ordering your books on the subject of MIB, and I am wondering if there are any cases of people actually making physical contact with these things. I have a theory about these beings, as well as the UFO phenomenon, Bigfoot-entities (except for Orang Pendek; that one I believe may be fleshy), lake monsters, Tricksters, etc. I'm not some New Age nut who claims to feel 'vibes,' but I don't need a crystal ball to know those things I encountered were screwing with me. The more uncomfortable I became, the stranger they acted. Like they were sadistically enjoying my torment. Anyway, I will read your books and will definitely let you know if I hear anymore 'plausible weirdness' around this area. Thank you again."

19

"The scene shows a large woman dressed in black"

What was, and still remains, one of the most fascinating and unsettling stories of a Woman in Black surfaced in the latter part of 2010, but had its origins decades earlier; specifically in the 1920s. It was a story of truly mind-blowing and surreal proportions, one which involved swirling tales of time-travel and none other than the legendary actor-director, Charlie Chaplin!

The strange saga began in October 2010. That was when old and grainy footage that was connected to Chaplin's 1928, silent movie, *The Circus* surfaced. Rather incredibly, the film-footage in question appears to show nothing less than a black-garbed woman, holding a cell-phone to her ear -- while doing her utmost to ensure her identity is hidden from the camera that was filming her – something of which she was, clearly, acutely aware. Not only that, there is something profoundly unsettling about the WIB, too, as will soon become apparent. First, however, some vital background data to set the scene.

Chaplin's movie starred the man himself as a circus clown who can only make people laugh by accident, rather than on cue. Although *The Circus* was a huge, financial success – it remains to this day the seventh most grossing silent-movie of all time – it was a production utterly blighted by bad luck and ill-omen. As we have seen time and again, where negativity and darkness lurk, so do the Women in Black.

During the course of the production of *The Circus*, Chaplin had the Internal Revenue Service on his back. His mother, who, in a deranged state, had spent years confined to a variety of nightmarish asylums, passed away. The studio in which the movie was made caught fire – almost disastrously so - something which set back filming by four weeks. The film negative was found to be scratched, but was eventually and skillfully restored. And, to cap it all, Chaplin was served divorce papers by his second wife, Lita Grey. It was after all of this mayhem and torment was over that a WIB decided to put in an appearance of the chilling kind. Her timing was appropriate for a breed of creature that seems to thrive on torment, disaster, and misfortune.

Captured on film and creepy as hell
- -

The Woman in Black in question does not appear in *The Circus* itself, but in footage that was taken outside of Mann's Chinese Theater, Hollywood, where Chaplin's movie had its premiere. It was footage added as an "extra" to a DVD release of *The Circus*. One of those who purchased and watched that extra footage was an Irish man named George Clark. As he watched the extra material, Clark saw something jaw-dropping and amazing. It was so unusual that, on October 20, 2010, he uploaded the film to his YouTube page, along with a commentary from himself which went as follows:

"This short film is about a piece of footage I found behind the scenes in Charlie Chaplin's film *The Circus*. Attending the premiere at Manns Chinese Theatre in Hollywood [California] - the scene shows a large woman dressed in black with a hat hiding most of her face, with what can only be described as a mobile phone device - talking as she walks alone. I have studied this film for over a year now - showing it to over 100 people and at a film festival, yet no one can give any explanation as to what she is doing. My only theory - as well as many others - is simple…a time traveler on a mobile phone. See for yourself and feel free to leave a comment on your own explanation or thoughts about it."

People did exactly that. And they did much more, too: The film briefly became an Internet sensation and was quickly picked up on by numerous media outlets throughout the world. At the time of writing, the short piece of film has had close to seven million viewings – and that's just on YouTube alone; never mind all the additional blogs and websites that have picked up on it. As for what the film shows, that's pretty much straightforward: An elderly woman, dressed entirely in black, walking passed the theater, which is displaying a prominent poster advertising Chaplin's production. Although the footage only lasts for a few seconds it is deeply curious – and for no less than several, extremely odd reasons.

The woman's large, black hat is pulled down tight around her head, to the extent that it appears she is doing her utmost to hide her face from the camera, something which she skillfully achieves. The collar of her coat - the only part of her attire that is not black - is turned up high, something which further helps to obscure her face. Her coat is long and black. As for her shoes, not only are they black; they are pointed and long to the point of almost appearing ridiculous; one might even be inclined to say they are witch- or crone-like. Now we come to the most important part of the story: The woman is clearly holding something to her left-ear – and in her left-hand. It looks to be nothing less than a small cell-phone. It, too, along with her hand, additionally helps to mask the woman's identity and appearance from the camera.

Cell-phones in the 1920s?

It almost goes without saying that down-to-earth explanations have been offered for this profoundly unusual piece of film. One of the very first things suggested was that the device in the woman's hand was a 1924 product of Siemens, something the company itself describes as "a compact, pocket sized carbon microphone/amplifier device suitable for pocket instruments."

Siemens adds: "For a while, the carbon amplifier patented by Siemens played a major role in hearing aid technology and significantly raised the volume of hearing aids. The electrical energy controlled by the carbon microphone was not fed to the receiver directly. It first drove the diaphragm of an electromagnetic system connected to a carbon-granule chamber. Current was transmitted across this chamber from the vibrating diaphragm electrode to the fixed electrode plate. The amplified current produced mechanical vibrations in the electromagnetic hearing diaphragm that were then transmitted to the ear as sound."

Another suggestion was that the perceived "cell-phone" was actually a Western Electric Company 34A carbon hearing aid, which was first manufactured in 1925. Western Electric notes that it "...marketed these early hearing aids under the 'Audiphone' trade name. It was one of the few 1-piece carbon hearing aids of the time. The unit measured 7¾" by 4" by 1½" and weighed just under 2 lbs. when fitted with batteries."

This is all well and good and would, to a significant degree, explain things, were it not for one critical issue. A careful, close-up analysis of the footage makes it undeniable that the Woman in Black is doing something that, thus far, I have not mentioned. She is clearly...*talking into the device.*

Both the Siemens and the Western Electric Company devices were designed to amplify sound for people who were hard of hearing. Neither of them had the ability – at all, in any shape or fashion - to broadcast the voice of the user to another, similar or identical device, in the way that our cell-phones do today. Plus, it's clear from watching the film that the Woman in Black is walking the street alone, so she cannot be speaking with a friend or relative next to her. The only other person in the film is a man who is clearly unconnected to her and who moves out of sight before she even starts speaking. This leaves only one option: whatever the nature of the device the woman is clutching tightly to her ear, it is designed to both receive and send communications of the verbal kind, and over a significant distance.

WIB or MIB?

There is one other anomaly, too: the size of the woman's feet, coupled with her very stocky, rotund form, gave rise to the theory that she might actually have been a man in disguise – something which took the affair to even weirder levels of surreal strangeness. What is even stranger is that there are more than a few reports on file of Women in Black that were actually suspected of being well-camouflaged MIB. Yes, the weird is about to become the downright bizarre.

Neil Arnold, a good friend of mine who has taken a keen interest in WIB reports, offers us the following:

"The *New York Times* of November 10th 1886 speaks of 'The Woman In Black – A Queer Character That Is Causing A Sensation In Scranton (Pennsylvania).' The newspaper commented that, 'For more than a week timid and superstitious persons throughout the city have been kept in a constant state of trepidation by the appearance in various places and at unseasonable hours of an uncanny figure that is now quite generally spoken of as 'The Woman In Black.'"

"Others believed the apparition to be a man dressed up"

Arnold continues: "The article added that, 'Two young women saw the sinister figure in the Pine Brook area after making their way home from a Saturday night 'hop.' The figure approached the women but spoke no words and gave off an air of malevolence. The young women were so horrified that they fled but the eerie woman overtook one of the women and hugged her. The terrified woman almost fainted. Her friend came to her aid but the mysterious figure in black vanished in a flash. The newspaper also goes on to mention that a few evenings previous a workman employed at the Lackawanna Iron and Coal Company had rushed to tell his colleagues that he'd seen a strange woman in black hiding in a lumber pile near the bank of the Roaring Brook.'"

The article, a copy of which was provided to me by Arnold, adds the following, which gets to the crux of the matter: "Upon investigation several men claimed to have seen a figure in black rushing towards the river from the direction of the lumber pile. A few men thought they could apprehend the woman but saw her leap into an abandoned mine. Armed with lamps the same men descended into the cave but could not find the woman. After the panic many surmised that the figure may well have been a demented local woman but *others believed the apparition to be a man dressed up* [italics mine]."

"I had an idea that she was a boy got up to frighten people"

Moving onto January 1893, there was a spate of WIB activity in Rhinebeck, New York. One Gus Quirk, described as an "ex-constable" from the village, decided to look into the matter of the WIB himself – chiefly because her spectral, crone-like appearance was proving fear and sleepless nights all around the neighbourhood. It's decidedly notable that the appropriately named Quirk said: "I won't stand any monkey business. I've got my suspicions. Of course they are merely suspicions and are based on what I think, but when it comes to a thing of this kind I usually think pretty nearly right thoughts. *I have thought that this woman in black was no woman at all. I had an idea that she was a boy got up to frighten people* [italics mine]. We have several boys in this village who are just about her height. I cross-questioned them pretty closely and I thought

I had hit the nail on the head, but one of the villagers came in just then and shouted: 'She's been seen not more than 10 minutes ago on the river road!' Of course my suspicious persons had proved an alibi without saying a word."

"At first we thought it was a man dressed up"

Of a recent case from Blue Bell Hill, Kent, England – which involved a couple who had the distinct misfortune to cross paths with a spectral WIB - Arnold quotes what they told him: "We turned icy cold. *At first we thought it was a man dressed up* [italics mine] but now I don't know what it was. It stood on the side of the road and was beckoning us (another feature which seems common in such encounters) with a bunch of heather in its hand but I'm sure it wasn't a gypsy.'"

Note, too, the near-identical wording of "a man dressed up" in both the account given to Arnold and that reported by the *New York Times* in 1886.

Whatever the true nature of the person in that priceless piece of footage – WIB or cross-dressing MIB - when the story of Charlie Chaplin, the mysterious woman, and the attendant film-footage surfaced, one common thread was ever-present in the discussion. Namely, the theory that the WIB was nothing less than a time-traveler. Just maybe, that's exactly what she was. And she may not have been a solitary time-surfer, either. It's time for *us*, too, to surf time: to the late 1930s.

<u>20</u>

"Maybe they decided it was too far advanced for people"

If the 1920s-era story of the possibly time travelling, cell-phone-using Woman in Black was not enough to amaze and intrigue, there is a near-identical story, from 1938, which involves a woman dressed in white. It's a story which hit the news in 2012; two years after the Charlie Chaplin saga exploded. In this case, however, the individual causing all the mystery was a Woman in White, a WIW. The controversy began – but was initially overlooked, to a significant degree – in 2012, when a brief piece of old black and white footage was uploaded to YouTube. It appeared to show something amazing: a young woman speaking into a cell-phone! Sounds familiar? Shades of the Charlie Chaplin/WIB saga? Yes, indeed.

The footage is undeniably genuine. The big question, however, is what does it show? What can be said for sure is that the WIW is holding something small and black to her ear. And she does appear to be speaking into it and engaging in conversation, all with a beaming smile on her face. As for the location, it has been identified as a Dupont factory in Leominster, Massachusetts. There's no doubt at all about the place.

It's important to note that the cell-phone, as a concept and then as an initial design, did not come to the fore until the early 1970s – thanks to the pioneering work of Motorola. And, it was not until the early 1980s that the first commercially available cell-phones went on sale. They were brick-sized, cumbersome things that today, look far more comical and absurd than they do revolutionary.

"They were experimenting with wireless telephones"

Among the fairly small community of people that tracks alleged sightings of time-travelers, the debate as to what the footage showed rumbled on quietly. That all changed in 2013, when the world's media – and I do mean the *world's* – latched onto the story, the film went viral, and all sorts of theories and thoughts were trotted out to try and explain what it showed.

The story that was given most publicity came via a source identified only as "Planetcheck," a YouTube user who claimed that the woman in the film was her great-grandmother, said to be named Gertrude Jones. Planetcheck said: "I asked her about this video and she remembers it quite clearly. She says Dupont had a telephone communications section in the factory. They were experimenting with wireless telephones. Gertrude and five other women were given these wireless phones to test out for a week. Gertrude is talking to one of the scientists holding another wireless phone who is off to her right as she walks by."

There are, however, problems with the claims of Planetcheck. First and foremost, she is wholly anonymous and has never come forward under her real name. Second, "Gertrude Jones" has never been formally identified. It would have been an easy thing to present evidence of Jones' existence, and have the matter laid to rest very quickly. Rather ironically, the media – which is usually highly dismissive when the UFO research community relies upon anonymous sources – immediately embraced the words of Planetcheck and practically cited them as established fact, which they clearly were not. Moreover, despite the words of the anonymous YouTube user, no "scientist" can be seen, anywhere, in the film, using "another wireless phone who is off to her right."

The secrets of the glass box

There are other issues, too: the original posting to YouTube showing Planetcheck's words was mysteriously removed – but not before both Yahoo News and the U.K.'s *Daily Mail* newspaper copy-pasted her comments and saved them for posterity and publication, which included the following: "Maybe they decided it was too far advanced for people and they abandoned the idea. Ideas are hatched, prototypes are made and sometimes like this phone they are forgotten until somebody discovers some long lost film of the world first wireless phone and marvels at it."

Then there is the outlandish claim of Planetcheck that the family still has the device, stored in what was described as a "glass box." This is, clearly, absurd. If DuPont *was* testing some sort of early cell-phone way back in 1938, then the chances are that it − or they, depending on how many devices were made − would have been tested within the confines of the facility. Staff would certainly not have been allowed to take them home, or even keep them. Such a scenario is ridiculous. It speaks volumes that Planetcheck didn't simply take a photo of the device in its box, and uploaded it to YouTube for all to see.

In addition, there are the words of David Mikkelson, the founder of Snopes.com. He said, quite correctly: "You can take any piece of WWII footage showing someone holding something to the side of their head talking, and claim it is a time traveling cell phone user. Film clips aren't of sufficient resolution to see what the people are carrying. It could be anything from a handkerchief to a hearing aid, or who knows what. And this video is silent, so you can't even tell if the person is engaged in a two-way conversation."

Although highly skeptical of the whole affair, Mikkelson made two valid points, which echo my words above: "I doubt it would have just been handed out to a young woman working at the factory. And why isn't there documentation?" Mikkelson's question is an important one, as there is no evidence that, back in 1938, DuPont was working on wireless telephones and was dishing them out to its employees – even to the extent of letting them take them home!

Today, Planetcheck has vanished and DuPont does not care to comment on the matter at all. Thus, we are left with – as we are with the saga of the WIB in the Charlie Chaplin footage – enigmatic footage of a woman giving every impression of speaking into a hand-held device, of a kind we are told was not developed until decades later.

<u>21</u>

"This scary-looking woman was tall and thin, had a face powdered white"

No book on the Women in Black would be complete without far more than a passing reference to a certain, hit movie of 2012 that starred a man who came to fame as a schoolboy-wizard. You have probably already guessed the name of the movie and the actor at issue. If you have not, however, I refer you to an excellent paper on the matter penned by Neil Arnold. It demonstrates truth is not just stranger than fiction, but that, from time to time, the two cross paths and intertwine in the strangest of ways. Over to Arnold, who wrote the following paper – "The Woman in Black" - in 2011, and who generously shared it with me so that I could share it with you:

"During the autumn of 2010 it was announced that *Harry Potter* star Daniel Radcliffe had landed a lead role in *The Woman In Black*, written by Jane Goldman and to be directed by James Watkins. This film, an adaptation of Susan Hill's classic ghost story, which was published by Puffin in

1983, will be of great interest to anyone with an eye for the lure of the sinister. Hill's atmospheric book is set in the village of Crythin Gifford, which harbours the Gothic Eel Marsh House. These foreboding premises sit on treacherous marsh, separated from land by a causeway which floods at certain times, leaving the looming house isolated from the outside world. The book introduces us to Arthur Kipps, a young solicitor sent to the property of the now deceased Alice Drablow. After attending the funeral of Mrs Drablow and spending a couple of nights in the old dark house, Kipps succumbs to night terrors and is plagued by a wandering spirit adorned in black. The wasted ghoul haunts him until the book reaches a tragic climax involving his wife and child.

"*The Woman In Black* is a ghost story with all the creaking quality of those antiquated tales told many years ago by the likes of M.R. James. Often simply suggestive of its horrors, one finds them self-enshrouded by the marsh mists and frozen by the chills. A few years after the book was published, Herbert Wise directed the film of the same name. It appeared on late night television one Christmas Eve and has become an obscure classic since then, never again seeing the light...or dark! Running for 99 minutes and with a few extra twists on Hill's book, the movie never gained the respect of the book, in fact those involved in the book and the stage production have rarely mentioned the film, as if to remain distanced from it. This is unfortunate because the film, which is well acted and excellently scripted, provides plenty of chills, especially when during one particular night Arthur Kidd (as he is known in the film) wakes to the leering face of the female apparition. (On Demand now carries the movie.) Several scenes on the marsh involving the darkly adorned crone are truly heart-stopping, and the shattering climax, an alternative take on the book's ending, is eerie to say the least.

"In 1987 playwright Stephen Mallatratt, achieved the impossible, by taking Hill's book to the stage. Whilst such a concept may have been sneered at by critics at the time, *The Woman In Black* now exists as one of the longest running London plays, with production from Peter Wilson. The *Daily Telegraph* called the play, 'The most brilliantly effective spine chiller you will ever encounter....If you haven't seen this show you are missing a treat,' whilst the *Sunday Mirror* commented, 'Don't go unless you like being scared out of your wits.'

"The biggest question was: how on earth could this bone-shuddering story work on stage, especially as Mallatratt had included only two actors for the stage? Director Robin Herford was unsure as to how a story, originally involving almost a dozen characters could be adapted for the stage. However, with the effective lighting of Kevin Sleep, and clever yet simplistic stage design by Michael Holt, *The Woman In Black* came to life, and took its first tentative steps onto the stage at the Lyric Theatre in Hammersmith. The play, due to some kind, but not excitable reviews, then transferred to the Strand, then the Playhouse, and finally found its home in 1989 at the Fortune Theatre, at Russell Street, Covent Garden. Who would have thought that this tiny theatre would enable the original ghost story to become a West End legend, and one so effective as to outshine (and out-creep) Susan Hill's book.

Nick Redfern with Women in Black authority, Neil Arnold. (Nick Redfern, 2009).

"Not only does the Fortune Theatre, in all its musty glory, allow the play to unfold like some ancient manuscript, but the rich script and stunning performances by varying actors over the years, have kept the story refreshing. As already mentioned, the theatrical version of the tale involves only two actors, well, three if you count the 'vision', but it has enough twists and turns, as well as creaks, and screams, to terrify even the most hardened of souls. This time however, we are narrated the story by a fumbling elderly gent, eager to have his story told, and which is played out by a younger actor. Their camaraderie is occasionally punctuated by the ghoulish appearance of the dreadful woman, who on one occasion seems to glide silently from nowhere, down the aisle and between the unsuspecting audience! With foggy effects, minimal lighting, and a cleverly constructed stage acting as haunted house, pub, train compartment, causeway, and graveyard, the mind of the audience works overtime in the gloom, every audible thud causing the heart to skip a beat, the gasps from those who look on being the only sound to emerge from the rows."

"Interestingly, the Fortune Theatre, whether by some bizarre coincidence, or peculiar manifestation, has its own ghost story or two – one being that of a woman in dark garments! Previous members of the cast, mainly Sebastian Harcombe, experienced two strange episodes, the first several years ago as the ghastly apparition of the story appeared during the first graveyard scene. Sebastian, looking towards the woman in black, saw two figures on the right of the stage, whilst the actress at the time mentioned also that she'd been followed, by a woman in black, as she made her way to the stage. Sebastian also saw a grey figure, possibly a woman, lurking in one of the lower boxes of the theatre.

"For those of a nervous disposition, it isn't the haunting that one should be concerned about in the place, but indeed the impact of the actual show – particularly the minimalist yet atmospheric stage, and the rare glimpses of the dreaded woman herself. *The Woman In Black* is the perfect Halloween or Christmas ghost tale. Whilst it looks as if it will remain embedded within Convent Garden's history for many years to come, it seems as if the ghosts it has unintentionally raised will remain only half-glimpsed, and less terrifying. Hopefully.

"When the play was put on at the Theatre Royal in Margate, in Kent it seemed once again that the legend had come to life. The Theatre Royal is Britain's second oldest theatre and is said to be rife with ghosts. One of these made its presence known in 1990 when *The Woman In Black* was staged. Actor Derek Waring claimed he'd seen a figure of a woman sitting in the stage box – an area out of bounds for many years. Not only has the section of theatre gathered dust over the years it has also gathered a reputation for being very haunted. The door of the area has been heard to slam with an almighty bang on many occasions. Some believe the ghost to be a Miss Sarah Thorne who lived next door to the theatre and was an actress who eventually became manager, her association with the theatre lasting for more than forty-five years. Usually when the female phantom appears lights in the theatre begin to flicker.

"Reports of ghostly women in black are often as vague

yet as common in folklore as sightings of grey ladies, white ladies, and grey and black monks. However, the following set of tales may shed some light on where Susan Hill drew inspiration for her ghastly main character.

"For instance. *The Morning Herald* of December 9th 1887 reported, 'The Ghost Found – And It Turns Out To Be A Poor Demented Woman', after reports in Atlanta, Georgia of a mysterious woman in black had plagued local residents. The woman, said to have a pale face 'now and then appeared on a trestle on the belt road, near where it crosses the Georgia Pacific.'

"According to local railroad workers every time the woman appeared a terrible disaster would take place – this is echoed in the book, film and stage play - and when anyone dared approach the woman she would simply vanish. Some people believed the sinister wraith to be a witch, but according to the newspaper, 'Friday morning the "ghost" was found lying in a pool of water unconscious and nearly frozen to death…the woman was evidently not sane.'

"The woman claimed her name was Annie Garrett and that she had become disgusted with the world and so decided to go and live in the woods – hence her disheveled appearance. Her ability to seemingly vanish when people approached was explained by a hole under the trestle in which she had probably slept.

"Bizarrely, when I was a child I distinctly recall a similar local woman who would walk the streets, close to home in Medway, and also more remote village lanes, adorned in black. This scary-looking woman was tall and thin, had a face powdered white, wore a silver headband and wore a black dress. Sometimes she would be seen dragging a bush or would simply walk down a busy street warning people to stay out of her way. Many recall this peculiar woman and some claim she lost a child when she was younger and so she roamed the streets, tormented by her past. Some say she was simply insane but was eventually cured and went on to live a happy life. Others believed she was a ghost. Whatever the answer, there's no doubt that any type of 'woman in black' is a scary sight especially when you least expect to see one, whether they are hoaxer, unhinged, or spectral.

"Hundreds of ghost stories pertain to women in black, but there needs to be a certain level or eeriness for such a specter to make a headline, or indeed cast an aura similar to that emitted by the sinister ghoul in Susan Hill's book and the theatrical version. On January 23rd 1950 the *Spokane Chronicle* spoke of a case from Bristol, in England, concerning a Reverend Francis J. Maddock and his task of exorcising a property at Highworth Road rumored to have been haunted by an old lady in black with a halo around her head.

"On August 19th 1892 the *Canaseraga Times* reported on the 'Woman In Black', with a lengthy chilling story concerning a train driver who'd seen a huge figure of a woman in black whilst traveling along a track one dark and stormy night. The figure appeared out of the gloom and appeared to be waving its arms (similar in fashion to the ghostly omen recorded in Charles Dickens' classic ghost story *The Signalman*) and contorting before disappearing into the night. His fellow driver never saw the figure but noted the expression of horror on the face of his colleague. A few moments later both men saw the hideous figure and they screeched the train to a juddering halt. Of course, there was no terrifying ghoul to be seen now, just the conductor asking what on earth was going on. All three men walked along the track and to their horror, but also their relief, they noticed just a few feet away the yawning chasm of the frothing river. And there, in the distance floating in the air was that chilling apparition, still flailing its arms.

"However, whilst it appeared that the terrible entity had indeed saved the lives of those on board the train, a passenger, a young boy was quick to point out, 'There's your woman in black!' The train driver recalled, 'And there it was, sure enough – that same moth miller that you see there in that frame. He was clinging to the inside of the glass. As I tapped on the glass the creature flew back and lighted up the reflector. That's the whole story, sir. The moth, by fluttering on the glass just in front of the electric glass just in front of the electric illuminator, had produced a great black shadow, like that of a cloaked woman, on the darkness in front of us; and when he flopped his wings in vain attempt to sail out through the glass, he gave his mysterious shadow the look of waving its arms wildly. Then when he flew back out of the direct shine of the light, the figure disappeared, of course. Anyhow, he saved our lives by scaring us with that Woman In Black…'

"*The Evening Independent* of June 17th 1926 reported, 'Prince Of Wales May Organize Ghost Hunt For The Black Lady Of Windsor Castle'. The woman in black was said to be the spirit of Queen Elizabeth and the ghost hunt would be organized to entertain the guests, including King George and Queen Mary. The figure was said to have appeared in time for Ascot week although the newspaper reports that, 'Intimates among the royal family generally, and attaches, and servants at the castle are maintaining silence concerning the apparition. They do not wish to frighten unromantic or timid guests, and are also a little ashamed to confess that they believe, as many do, that the ghost really appeared.'

"The woman in black, although non-threatening, was said to often appear at night. Her first 'authentic' appearance was said to have taken place in 1897 and was witnessed by Lieutenant Carr Glyn of the grenadier guards. According to the Lieutenant the woman wore a black, medieval dress and veil over her face. She walked by him and disappeared into an adjacent room.

"There is a festive story concerning a woman in black. *The Calgary Herald* of December 22nd 1950 reported 'British Ghost May Return To Its Haunts', after sightings at the old Yattendon Rectory in Berkshire of a headless phantom clad in black. Rev. Alec Farmer, the rector of Yattendon told newspapers that the figure usually appears when there is a Christmas party spirit in the air and she often appears between the kitchen and the servants' quarters. The woman was said to have lost her head a couple of centuries previous. Twelve years later the *Reading Eagle* reported on a figure in black seen near St. Patrick's cemetery in Gallitzin, Pennsylvania. On this occasion the black ghost was confronted by a one Edward Reagan who asked, "What are you trying to prove ?" and the mysterious specter fled.

"Of course, only a handful of such alleged hauntings can hold a candle to the horrors of the creaking ghost story created by author Susan Hill. However, whether it's the little known Western Massachusetts specter in black of 1871, or the hazy legend of a disheveled, wild eyed woman said to haunt your local remote lane, there's no doubting the power of such a figure…and that candle they hold may come in useful after all. And let us hope that when the film was released in 2012 the ghostly legend lived up to expectations.

For many, it did exactly that.

22

"I have never felt such fear in my life"

Christina George is the founder of the Psychic Paranormal Research Society, and someone who had a truly disturbing encounter in 2012 that blended the worlds of UFOs and the supernatural into one terrifying cocktail. It's a story that is focused on a strange and disturbing woman, and her equally odd children. And with that said, I will hand over the reins to Christina, who told me the following:

"Back in the summer of 2012 myself and a few members of my paranormal group, here in Sacramento, went up to see a client about a report of being abducted. He was claiming he had an implant and was experiencing paranormal activity; this was in Redding, California. We finished up our investigation and headed back home.

"When I got home, it was early in the afternoon and we decided – my roommate and I – we were going to go to the grocery store real quick and then come back. And the sub-division that we lived in had just one entrance; a cul-de-sac; it wrapped around and there was a little street that branched off the cul-de-sac area. It ended up at a dead-end at a green belt. That is where my home was. So, we went to the store, and I was talking to my roommate about all the weird things that had happened in the case and as we pull back to our home, we saw three people standing on our property."

As Christina notes, this is where things got very weird and unsettling:

"It was almost like they were kind of waiting for us; they were standing in a row. So, I asked my roommate if he knew who they were. We looked at each other and he said, 'Who's that?' and I said, 'I have no idea.' Now, you have to understand that my roommate was somebody who really did not like unexpected visitors, solicitors; anything like that. So, seeing these people was a little strange."

Also strange was the appearance of the creepy trio, as Christina makes abundantly clear:

"One thing that I noticed when we pulled up was that the reason why they really looked out of place was there was one woman who was a Caucasian; she had longish brown hair, like she hadn't combed it in a while. And she had a mismatched outfit on for summertime and it was all wrinkly. And then I noticed she had two children with her.

"Both children had mismatched clothing on. Shorts and a t-shirt but they didn't go together. They were very, *very* pale-skinned. One was a little African-American girl and her hair didn't look combed and her skin was very dry. I noticed that right away. And then I looked at the little boy, and I didn't really know if he was a Caucasian child, or if he was an African-American with albinism. This child, his skin was white as milk. It was very, very white. He had these strange blue eyes; I had never seen such a shade of blue eyes before. It was something that stood out to me."

The anxiety levels of Christina and her roommate began to rapidly rise.

"I got this really, really strange connection"

"I thought: I wonder who these people are? We don't have homeless people who wander around the area, so it was very out of place. I thought maybe they were homeless, or she was a foster-parent. My roommate was kind of perturbed that not only were they at our house, but they were standing on our property. So, he pulled up to the garage, into the driveway, and turned off the car and got out, closes the door and walks over there really fast. I see him cross his arms and I can see that he's talking to them, but I can't hear them; I can only see them through the window."

It was then that things took a very unusual turn; almost as if Christina's roommate had been placed into some hypnotic trance:

"Right about this time, I see that he drops his arms to his sides, he turns around, he walks back and gets in the car, closes the door, pulls in the garage, pulls the garage door down; never says anything to me. And I said, 'Who were they? What did they want?' And he said, 'Oh, don't worry about it; they're looking for some lost feral kittens.' Now, just for myself, I thought: lost feral kittens? First of all, how do you know there are lost feral kittens over here, and, why in the world would you be looking for them?"

She noted that her roommate's odd behavior only increased:

"He gets out of the car, closes the door, and walks into the house. And we lived in a tri-story home. So, when you walk in, that was our main floor. You would go downstairs; that's where the bedrooms were. And upstairs we had the kitchen and things like that. So, he goes in his bedroom and he closes the door. He leaves me in the car, in the garage, and I'm just sitting there, still trying to process this whole lost feral kitten scenario. It doesn't make any sense to me. And the fact that he took that excuse, as well, was baffling me even more. And that he just got up and left, as if we weren't even having this conversation."

Christina then decided it was up to her to take some action:

"I get out of the car and I put my stuff upstairs, and it was really bothering me. So, the investigator, or nosey person, that I am got the best of me. I decided I was going to go down and peek and see if these people were still out there. I go to the main floor and I have these big plantation shutters. I go to try and peek out these things and I see all three – the lady and the two children. They are no longer standing on my grass. Now, they are on the side of my house, where it overlooks a hill that goes down to a creek bed. They are all standing in a line. And, when I'm looking at them, there was such a strange energy that I felt. But, all of a sudden, I got this really, really strange connection; like an energy."

It was then that something not just chilling, but almost *beyond* chilling, happened.

```
"I have this fear that comes over me"
```

"All three of them, in unison, turned from the waist back and looked dead at me, as if they knew I was looking at them. It was almost like robotic. All three did it at the exact same time, and it startled me. But, not only did it startle me, one of the things I was looking at, I locked eyes with them."

They were eyes of what can only be described as a non-human type:

"And I look in them, and all I could see was just black. I remember seeing them originally, and I could tell the lady had lighter brown eyes, and the little African-American girl, she had darker brown eyes. But you could see the whites of their eyes. All I could see, now, was complete black. I even looked at the little boy, because I'm thinking, he was a little faraway and I'd not seen him up close. But I look at this little boy and, again, complete black. It almost made their eyes look bigger, like the eyelid wasn't closed over it; very prominent. I lock eyes with them.

Christina George: "I have never felt such fear in my life."
(Christina George, 2016).

"I will tell you I have never felt such fear in my life. Now, I have been able to see and interact with spirits my whole life, since childhood, and I have investigated the paranormal the majority of my life, and publicly and professionally for the past twelve years. I had never really encountered anything that scared me the way this did. So, I have this fear that comes over me and I try to let go of the blinds so they can't see me, and I jump back. I'm thinking, oh my God, what did I just see? Is this real? I tried to get myself together, and the first thing I think of is: I need a witness. Who do I think of? My roommate.

"I go running down the stairs and I start banging on his door, and I'm trying to open the door; the door's locked. And, I'm listening and I hear water running, like the shower running. I'm banging on the door, screaming for him to come out. And he doesn't come out.

"At this point, I ran back up the stairs, and I'm standing there and, if you picture this in your mind, for me it was very terrifying. But, I'm the person who never gets scared of the paranormal stuff. I'm the big leader of our group. I speak on the paranormal. And here I was, running around like I needed someone to help me. I'm thinking, what do I do? So, after a few minutes, I have to settle myself; I'm talking to myself, literally saying: what are you doing? This is what you do for a living: are you kidding me? Get it together! So, I decide that I'm going to look outside again."

It was an action on Christine's part that once again provoked nothing but stone-cold fear.

"I'm thinking all this chanting is wrong"

Christina continues: "I go to the blinds again; I peek out and I look at the spot where they were before and I don't see them. I pan over to the left and over back to where they were before, and, lo and behold, they are right there. They're standing near a tree that's on my property and they were standing in a circle, holding hands, and they were rocking back and forth. I could see that – the two I could see from where I was at, directly – their mouths were moving, as if they were saying something, together. The little boy had his back to me, so I couldn't see what he was saying. But, it looked as if they were chanting or singing.

"I was trying to figure what they were doing and they stop, and all three of them – again – turn and look directly on me and lock in. And, so I jump back and almost fall down the stairs. I cannot believe what I have just seen. I'm thinking, why are they in a circle? What are they chanting? What are they saying? Why am I so scared? I run back downstairs again and I'm pounding on the door again; still hearing water running. He doesn't answer the door. I'm at the bottom of the door, and I'm thinking, pull yourself together. Why are you waiting? Ask them what's going on."

And that's exactly what Christina did:

"I got my courage up and I go upstairs, unlock the door, and pull it open, and forceful; like I'm going to go out there and demand to know what's going on. I shouted: 'What are you doing? What do you want? What are you doing on my property?' And they dropped hands and the lady turned and looked at me and said, 'Nothing; we're done.' And they started walking off the property and out of my view line, across where my garage is. And I was standing there, almost frozen, processing what they just said.

"I'm thinking all this chanting is wrong: what are they

all done with? I run down my walkway – which runs along-side my house and to where the garage is – and I look, and probably only literally a couple of seconds passed by. And I run out to the end and I didn't see them anywhere. I was thinking: did they run? Is this a joke?

"So, I decided I'm going to jump in my car and I'm going to head them off at the exit. As I'm running back into the house, my roommate is coming up the stairs. At the time, I look at him, scream about what happened, and we jump in my car and go zooming out and there's nobody. I go do the whole circle of the cu-de-sac and all the way around; nothing. I also saw some of the neighbors, as it was a weekend, and so I literally went house to house asking each of the neighbors: 'Did you see this lady and these two children?' Nobody had seen anybody come by. When the kids and the woman left, they would have to have passed by one of them, at least."

It was then that the air of weirdness that surrounded Christina's roommate returned:

"I asked my roommate, 'Why would you take a shower? I was trying to get your attention?' He said, 'I wasn't in the shower; I was in my room.' I said I was knocking on the door, and he said, 'No, you weren't.' It was crazy. It was like: what reality are we in? Now, I start questioning my sanity, at this point."

Then, that same night, there was a very eerie development:

"Throughout that evening, each of the investigators who were with me on our investigation up in Redding ended up calling me, independently, and said: 'Oh my gosh, you're not going to believe what just happened when I got home.' I said, 'I might!'

"Each of them were having some very strange occurrences, but we all agreed mine was definitely the strangest. It was like the Black Eyed Kids, but there were no hoodies or sweats and I wasn't alone. I'd never heard of a black-eyed adult, either. I had never thought to check on the area where they did the chanting, to see if there was any residual energy, something like that. We went out and only that area, in a circle, was literally spiking our EMF meter off the chart. I have had a lot of electronic interference in spikes. And phone calls with almost like chatter in the background. Almost like chirping, at times."

The trauma- and fear-filled event was over. Not surprisingly, however, Christina has not been able to forget it, years later. Nor is she likely to anytime soon.

A study of Christina's experience demonstrates a number of similarities between her experience and other WIB-themed events. For example, the speed with which Christina's roommate seemed to have been placed into a kind of docile, submissive state after speaking with the mysterious woman very much echoes the 1971 experience of President Richard Nixon's house-keeper, Shirley Cromartie, who was plunged into a mind-controlled state by a strange, wig-wearing MIB. That the woman and the children were standing on the doorstep, and when confronted came up with a feeble and nonsensical explanation (or, rather, excuse), namely that they were looking for feral kittens, is *also* typical behavior of both the WIB and the MIB. Then there is the matter of those black eyes.

The blackest eyes of all

Who, or what, the so-called Black Eyed Children are is a matter that has had the paranormal and UFO research communities occupied for several years. Before we get to the nature and potential intent of the BECs, let's first take a look at their appearance – which is, without doubt, eerie in the extreme. Typically, the BECs appear to range in age from around ten to fourteen. They are, more often than not, male. They are acutely skinny and pale in the extreme. Their preferred color of clothing is black, and almost always a black hoody that envelopes – and hides - most of their face. Then there is the matter of why they are named the Black Eyed Children. Put simply, their eyes are black. And we're not just talking about portions of the eye. No: the *entire eye* is black.

Their intent is curiously identical in practically every case on record: they try and find any way possible to enter the home or the vehicle of the person they target. Since most of the people who have encountered the BECs are terrified out of their wits by the appearances of their strange visitors, they seldom, if ever, allow them entry – which means we are pretty much at a loss to understand *why* it's so important for the BECs to gain access to peoples' property.

As for the theories for what the Black Eyed Children might be, they range from predatory vampires to energy-sucking ghosts, and from demonic beings to fairy-like changelings. It's important to note that unlike some of the hybrid children that alien abductees report encountering, there is simply no way that the BECs can pass amongst us unnoticed. The hybrid children may look somewhat strange and sickly, but they are not always overly alien-looking. The blank, black eyes of the BEC, however, effectively ensure that no one is going to come away from an encounter with them and think "sickly child." On top of that, the Black Eyed Children possess the disturbing ability to near-hypnotize people, as they attempt to enforce their malevolent will on their unfortunate victims.

And, just to reinforce matters, the WIB, the MIB, and the BEC all do their utmost to find a way into the homes of their victims – "victims" being a most appropriate term, as Christina George can certainly attest to.

23

"There was something 'off' about them"

Felix is someone who had a notable encounter with both a Woman in Black and a MIB midway through 2013. To put things in their correct context, however, it's important to note that Felix had an earlier, similar encounter in 1981. Felix's 1981 story is told in the pages of my 2015 book, *Men in Black: Personal Stories and Eerie Adventures*, which was my third book on the MIB, after *On the Trail of the Saucer Spies* and *The Real Men in Black*. I have, however, included it here, below, to help set the scene for what was to happen in 2013, and to demonstrate that sometimes witnesses can expect to experience follow-up encounters with the dark-clothed ones. With that said, over to Felix:

"I was woken by the sound and 'feel' of visitors"

"First of all, I'll set this account in context. I'm a transgender person - born female, living as androgyne and a natural psychic. My father was a practicing occultist; he was a member of the Golden dawn in the '50's and a lifelong student of magic and metaphysics. My mother attended a spiritualist church and had a number of experiences that assured her that the death of the physical body was not the end of the personality. I would describe myself as an eclectic occultist and researcher.

"I was brought up to accept there will always be phenomena that we may not understand and to be critical but not dismissive of anything odd that happened to me. I was born in 1954 and raised in Blackpool, from where I moved to Manchester in 1982 as a mature student, reading Theology and Comparative Religion.

"In 1981 I lived in an attic bedsit in one of the big, old houses that had been converted into flats. It was just one room, really with a Baby Belling cooker in a former wardrobe and a sink in the corner, providing hot water through a Creda. My bed was in a corner with the window behind me and to the right. The door was past the foot of the bed on the left hand wall.

"In December 1980 I had had a pregnancy terminated; this had been a stressful time, physically and mentally but I was coping OK. I wasn't working but had work as a bar supervisor lined up for the summer season so was taking it easy for a while.

"Now, in spite of my interest in matters mysterious, UFOs and alien contact have never particularly grabbed my attention. I'd read a little about claims of alien abduction but had no books on the topic and of course there was no internet back then.

"Very late one night in, I think, February 1981, I woke suddenly to see the semi-transparent form of a youth in 1930's type clothing, writing at the table under the window. He seemed unaware of me and I just thought, 'That's nice; he seems happy enough. I wonder if he's a spirit or a memory imprint on the house?' turned over and went back to sleep. I don't know how long after this I was woken by the sound and 'feel' of visitors.'"

"I was as if they held me in a trance or catatonic state"

"I sat up in bed and saw two men in the room, absolutely solid and 'real,' assumed they were police and wondered how the hell they had got in. I recall saying, 'What?' and they approached the bed. I lay down, grabbing the quilt in fright but they were absolutely impassive and did not address me directly. One took a gadget a bit like a mobile phone in appearance and 'scanned' me with it. He told his companion – I'm not sure whether I heard this with my ears or telepathically - that this was a female 20-30 years and was infertile due to contraception (or a term meaning the same). I had recently started using the Pill.

"The other man took a stroll around the room,

examining its contents. He seemed very amused by anything that plugged into the wall - the Creda heater and my radio-cassette (the latter is especially important) - and commented, smiling, 'I can't believe they're still harnessing it from an external source.' I felt that he was familiar with people generating their own electricity via their bodies. All the time this was going on I couldn't move or speak - it was as if they held me in a trance or catatonic state.

"The next thing I knew it was morning and I was alone. I reached down, shaken, to switch the radio on and was surprised to hear just a load of static. On inspection I saw it had been tuned to an area where there is NO station. Now, I always had it tuned to Radio 1 (a lot of young folk did then) and never touched it. It was the last thing I recall the man picking up. It wasn't until later that evening that I put together the pieces of the visit and thought, 'Men in Black!'"

"They looked odd and retro"

"In appearance they were very similar and dressed identically, like twins. Both around 5'8 – 5'9 in height with a slim build. Their complexion was a bit olive/jaundiced, eyes I'm not sure and what hair I could see was black. They wore beige, straight cut raincoats over dark trousers and shoes with white shirts and black ties and each had a beigey-brown fedora. They looked odd and retro and had an aura not of menace but of indifference to humans; I felt they looked at us as specimens in a laboratory.

"I have never told anyone but my parents this story and always had the feeling I was not meant to discuss it, at least for a number of years. As decades have passed, I thought I would share it with you. I hope you found it interesting!

"Again, many thanks for your excellent book on this topic – I'm presently torn between the tulpa and the time-traveler models but I'd rather they didn't come back to tell me. ;-)"

"I was met with the sight of two individuals, a male and female"

In November 2015, Felix sent me the following email, detailing her WIB/MIB encounter of 2013:

"I live on the 13th floor of a tower block of flats originally built as social accommodation for families in Manchester just after the war. The local council eventually sold them to a housing association and recently, due to Lottery money and other funding they have been radically improved beyond recognition. Security is very tight, with electronic entry systems front and back, CCTV, inner doors which can only be accessed with a tenant's key and, behind these the actual front doors of the individual flats, which are arranged in sets of three.

"Now, in order to view a property you have to apply

to the housing association using their official forms and provide ID in order to collect a set of keys to view at an arranged time. Usually a member of the association will come along, too.

"Around 18 months ago the flat across the hall from me became vacant after some rather sweet (but seriously in arrears) African students had to move out. It had stood empty for a few weeks after the caretaker had been in and done his stuff. One afternoon I was about to pop to the corner shop when I heard voices in the hall and thought I'd take the opportunity for a peek at any potential new tenants on the way out.

"On opening the front door I was met with the sight of two individuals, a male and female, both white and, I would estimate, in their early thirties. They were dressed as if they had come from an office - he in standard black suit and tie and she in a black skirt suit and white blouse. She had blonde, almost shoulder length hair and he had short brown hair, very neat and conservative. He was tall - a good six feet and looked like he could look after himself she was around five feet six and medium build. Both were healthy looking. Neither had any odd features; they just looked like an 'ordinary' couple but there was something 'off' about them. I couldn't quite put my finger on it. I wondered, in fact if they were plainclothes police officers, trying to pass themselves off as a couple.

"The woman, meanwhile, was staring and frowning"

"'Hi!' I said, smiling 'are you viewing the flat?' The woman said nothing but the man said, 'Er, yes.' He smiled back but the smile didn't reach his eyes. He reminded of those Scientologists you see in documentaries who exercise enormous control over their facial movements. Then he reached as if to put an arm around the woman but she looked uncomfortable and moved away. She looked me up and down, quite rudely like a young child might, then turned to look at the front door and asked, in a flat sort of voice, 'Is anyone in there, do you know?'

"'No,' I said, puzzled. 'The flat's empty, of course. They don't let them while tenants are still in! Don't you have keys?' 'Oh…yes!' said the man, as if the thought had just occurred to him. He cleared his throat and put his hand to his side as if to retrieve keys from his pocket. The woman, meanwhile, was staring and frowning at the front door and suddenly reached out a tentative hand towards it, for all the world as if she didn't know how it worked. It really was the most odd gesture - similar to the way a cat reaches out a paw when it's unsure of what it's seeing. 'Is no one meeting you?' I asked. They didn't answer; the woman looked nervous and disorientated, while her companion just stood there like a statue. 'Well, I'll leave you to it,' I said, 'Maybe see you later.' There was no response so I set off to the shop and left them to it. When I returned less than ten minutes later there was no one there and no signs of life from the vacant flat. I hadn't seen a car pull away or anyone walking from the building.

"They weren't a couple in any usual sense of the word"

"Well, there's no reason to suspect these were alien visitors or anything other than rather odd humans but, even apart from their seeming social awkwardness, the whole situation didn't ring true for people viewing a property. They would have received keys and been met by an agent from the housing association for a start – I've never known anyone be allowed to just wander about on their own in a vacant flat. If they didn't have keys how had they got into the hall? There was no one in the flat to answer the doorbell. There is a chance someone may have let them into the main part of the building if they had rung a number at random or followed someone in but the interior doors are fire doors and you have to use a key on them from the exterior side which no one but the housing association is allowed to make a copy of. They also didn't look like your average social housing tenant; they looked too professional, too middle-class but their behavior was almost autistic. And I swear - their body language was way off.

"Ah, well, it's these sort of incongruous events that keep

life interesting! Hope you enjoyed my little skirmish - I thought it might be your sort of thing! All the best, Felix."

Recall that references to autism appear in the 2008 story of "A Hesitant Believer."

<u>24</u>

"I had a very strange feeling when I saw the woman"

Denise Stoner is a woman with a notable background: she is the Director of the Florida Research Group affiliation of UFORCOP, a Mutual UFO Network National Abduction Research Team (ART) member, a Florida MUFON Field Investigator, a Star Team Member, and a former Florida MUFON, State Section Director, and Chief Investigator. She co-authored and published her first book *The Alien Abduction Files*, which was released in May of 2013. And, as you might surmise, she has had run-ins with the Women in Black – and with the MIB, too. Her intriguing story, told to me across 2013 and 2014, follows.

"He is watching me"

"At least three times here in Florida at a particular combination health/grocery/restaurant called *Whole Foods* I have been observed by a strange character. This is a good place to blend as many folks who shop here are 'odd characters' to begin with or 'hippie like,' gone back to nature types. So, the person who has observed me is wearing a gauzy outfit, thin hair, woven straw Panama type hat and sunglasses fits right in. His skin, hair, and clothing are all almost the same beige color.

"The difference is he has a drink in front of him, a notebook, stares at me the whole time as we eat at a table on the sidewalk. He never has food of his own nor does he touch the drink. It seems he knows when we are almost finished eating, he gets up, walks slowly past our table, rounds the corner that is clearly visible but must pass a pillar on the corner of the shopping plaza by our table. Once he goes behind that pillar, he never comes out the other side. There is literally nowhere for him to go but out the other side, then down the sidewalk or out to the parking lot - but no, he is gone. I cannot get up to follow thinking I am going to bump in to him on the other side of the pillar. He lets me know in no uncertain terms that he is watching me or letting me know he is there.

"Yes, I have pondered many times what prevents me from picking up my cell phone and taking a picture of this individual. I have no answer for that. It absolutely crosses my mind the whole time the episode is taking place. Afterwards I feel foolish, know I will be made fun of in the telling of the story, and promise myself I will have the camera ready the next time. It never happens. Are we somehow prevented from having photographic evidence needed as proof?

"I do have several speaking engagements a year and have decided to add one of these odd stories each time as I feel people need to know this type of thing exists. Let them decide for themselves what they think. This is going on and that is a fact - the fact appears to be that we have some type of 'human' with unusual abilities living among the earthly beings and our only choice for now is to be observant, to watch and wait. What other options do we have?"

And Denise has yet another account to relate, this one of mysterious men and women...

"The glass doors opened and two very tall, thin women entered"

"The situation has remained clear as crystal in my mind. As for my Mom, she knows something happened but it has gotten foggy and she doesn't know why, yet she recalls something happened that made her feel very uncomfortable.

"My Mom and I had gone to the mall on Christmas Eve for a couple of last minute stocking stuffer type gifts. We actually knew what we wanted so we parked outside J.C. Penney's on the side where those goods were. We went in and immediately noticed that in late afternoon, there were only a few shoppers. We picked out our gifts and got in line at the cashier in back of two other people. We could easily see the exit door and the sun in the parking lot, we were facing that way.

"The glass doors opened and two very tall, thin women entered. They had long almost waist length blond hair parted in the middle on top and it was thin in texture. Their skin was also pale and I did not notice any make up but each had huge piercing blue eyes. Their gait was odd like they were too tall (approximately 6'1) to walk smoothly. I was already an investigator for MUFON, so was aware of oddities in people and had done background searches for the Federal Government; I was trained to be observant.

"They were pushing one of those umbrella style strollers with no fancy attachments - just the hammock type bed, wheels, and handles. I noticed they had no purses or accessories such as a diaper bag to carry diapers or bottles, etc. The women moved slowly it seemed and drew my attention to the stroller. There was a baby blanket in the bottom portion and on top the head of a baby no bigger than a small grapefruit, pasty colored skin, no noticeable nose, a line for a mouth and huge dark eyes taking up most of the rest of this head.

"I wondered if the baby was deformed but knew this was not the case somehow. The baby appeared alert and was staring up at me. My Mom bumped me with her arm to get my attention and said 'what is wrong with that baby?' I felt I needed to tell the person in front of me because we had been talking with her about being slow in finishing up our shopping. When I tapped her on the shoulder, I was then shocked to see not only her, but the lady in front of her and the cashier, were kind of frozen in place. Everything seemed to be moving in extremely slow motion around us."

Denise Stoner: "I had a very strange feeling when I saw the woman." (Denise Stoner, 2016).

"We had been shown something in the store we both feel wasn't normal"

"The blond women seemed to pass the thought to me that I needed to take another good look at the baby and study it. Then as if a film was put back in to normal speed they walked past me and the cash register began to work, people - the only three in the area were moving again as if nothing happened.

"I told my Mom to hold our places and I ran after the women. Just next to us was the infants' clothing department. The women had turned in to that aisle. I followed and when I turned in to the aisle - they disappeared. Just gone like they had never been there. I ran back the short distance to my Mom and told her they were gone. We checked out and my Mom kept saying, 'what was going on with that baby?' I told her no one goes shopping with a baby that tiny without taking needed supplies, bottles, diapers, clothes, etc.

"I remember asking her if she thought we had seen something alien such as a hybrid and she just shook her head as if there was no answer. We stepped out the door and that's when the experience with the men took place.

"When we exited the mall my Mom had already stepped off the curb to locate my car, I was stopped by three men who were leaning on the brick wall by the door. Wearing black suits, black hats, white shirts, sunglasses. Short in stature. The only difference from your reports was the fact that one had a briefcase - black also. I don't recall their mouths moving but it could be I was just nervous.

"One of them said, 'you will not discuss what happened inside that store, do not talk about it to anyone; do you understand?' I did not answer, stepped off the curb as I felt I was in danger and called after my Mom. Just after I stepped off the curb I turned back to discover these men were gone and there was nowhere for them to go other than in to the parking lot or further down the sidewalk as there was a brick wall where they had been and continued down the length of the building to the only door we had come out.

"We had been shown something in the store we both feel wasn't normal and were talking about it as we left to see if we were imagining things when I met these men. Does this sound typical of these types? I am too old to be abducted and used for breeding and have had a hysterectomy so that could not have been the purpose - to show me a child of mine and I felt nothing like that was going on."

"She had shoulder length black hair with bangs, slightly tanned yet doughy looking skin"

Now we come to an encounter that Stoner had in 2014, which was of a full-blown Women in Black kind. Stoner reveals the strange saga, as follows:

"Around the time we were awakened from a rare afternoon nap by a man who said he was with the fire department here to inspect our smoke alarms - yet had no earthly idea what one was - we had another odd occurrence. Actually, it was two days later. Again, we were asleep very early in the morning just after sunrise. Our daughter enjoys sleeping on the sofa in the living- room Friday evening through Sunday evening because she can have her snacks, drinks, etc. on the table within arms' reach while she watches the big screen TV. She is disabled and lives with us. Although she could have her own place, she prefers staying in our home.

"The front door is across from her facing north and to the left. Three feet from the front door to the right we have a monitor with microphone that shows us in color what/who may be at the door and what cars are parked directly in front of our home and the home to our left. A huge doubly wide window is next and further right with wooden blinds closed most of the time. We live on one end of a T-shaped court - ours being the top of the T on the left side, once you turn the T upside down.

"Our dog sleeps in bed with us and this particular morning he did not wake up or move; my husband and I did not wake up. The doorbell was ringing and ringing and ringing like someone was playing a trick - a child, perhaps, and was going to run away when the door was answered. The strange thing was the fact that our dog did not bark and he should have at the first ring to warn us. I never heard it, my husband, who is a Viet Nam Vet, never heard it. Our master- bedroom is just left of the front door and we hear everything. Our daughter called to us and said 'Mom, you better come out here, there are two ladies with black clothes ringing the door bell and won't stop.' I jumped out of bed, now hearing the incessant ding-dong and beginning to figure one of our neighbors had an emergency. We all know each other and each one is willing to help out.

"I was no more than three or four seconds getting to the front door, my eyes already focusing on the monitor. There stood a woman who, to me, resembled a person of Native

American ethnic group, if I were to guess. She had shoulder length black hair with bangs, slightly tanned yet doughy looking skin, and dark, large black eyes looking straight in to the camera. I could see that she had on a black jumper style dress with thinner than normal straps running over her shoulders to the bib portion of the dress - almost suspenders minus the clips. She had on a long sleeved under blouse in a dark shade of grey."

A rendition of one of the Women in Black that terrified Denise Stoner. (Zachary P. Humway, 2016).

"I had a very strange feeling when I saw the
woman staring"

"Standing next to her was another woman identical to her in description only shorter in stature by a head. The height was difficult to judge due to the monitor, but she was not as tall as the lower portion of the camera, so I would say one was just over five-feet and the other just over four. I unlocked the door and swung it open only to discover there was no one there. Not a soul.

"I glanced down only seconds, just long enough to check the lock. My eyes were no longer on the monitor but the door and then the porch. Again, a matter of seconds. I am now looking at an empty porch, the house next door, an empty parking lot (I can identify all my neighbors' cars), grass walk-through on the left and right, and a sidewalk to the street straight ahead between two homes.

"There is no way possible these two women could get to any of these described places in the time I opened my front door. I would be able to see them walking or a car beginning to pull out of the lot or see them entering a home and there were no unidentified vehicles in the area. We are in a private subdivision with only one way in and one way out, the children are well behaved and are not seen playing outside without their parents present basically on Sunday afternoons. This is a very quiet undisturbed subdivision people are not even aware of and that is why we chose to live here."

Stoner concludes:

"I had a very strange feeling when I saw the woman staring in to the camera, looking in to the monitor as if she knew I was looking back. I felt uncomfortable and invaded somehow, as if I was given a warning but couldn't read or understand the language. So, this is the story of the female version of my experience. Very odd, yet just as disturbing as the MIBs. I have not heard of any others and can't wait to hear how this compares as the commonalities are important to those of us who experience these 'things.'"

25

"She shrank from him
with a hissing sound"

One of the strangest, and undeniably hair-raising, aspects of
the Women in Black phenomenon is their often-reported
propensity to hiss at people in menacing, and almost ani-
malistic, fashion. It's something that, until late 2015, I had
completely overlooked. Hence why, in terms of its chronol-
ogy, the story appears here.

Reports of these hissing WIB date back to at least the
19th century and extend to very recent years. The *Sunday
Herald* newspaper of January 13, 1893 told a disturbing tale
of an encounter with just such a WIB at Rhinebeck, New
York. The title of the article was "A Woman in Black." As for
the sub-title, it got straight to the paranormal point: "Like
Other Ghosts She is Only Seen at Night – Neither is She
Dumb, but Emits a Hissing Sound Which Startles the Ear
and Congeals the Blood."

According to the story, "a mysterious woman in black"
was provoking "much fear" in and around Rhinebeck. It's
hardly surprising when one takes note of what the *Sunday*

Herald had to say next: "It is the story of a strange creature who glides noiselessly along the country roads at dead of night. She has never been known to address anybody, although she has met many. Her language is the language of signs. She invariably halts long enough to stretch out her long arm from beneath a black veil and at the same time *make a hissing noise* [italics mine]."

"A tall black object standing perfectly still"

Adding to the state of terror in which the unfortunate witnesses found themselves plunged, the WIB was described as being "thin, at least six feet four inches tall, with a slight stoop and a long stride." Not the sort of woman to cross paths with on a dark night in 19th century Rhinebeck.

According to what newspaper staff learned of the hissing Woman in Black, she had first been seen around town roughly six weeks earlier – having previously haunted "the villages just north of Poughkeepsie." The first person in Rhinebeck who had the dubious honor of meeting the woman was John Judson, of Chestnut Street. His encounter was mercifully brief and involved the sighting of "a tall black object standing perfectly still." Terrified, Judson raced for home, arriving in a "cold sweat."

"She shrank from him with a hissing sound"

By the following day, said the *Herald*, the story was "all over Rhinebeck." Some laughed and others shivered, reported the newspaper. But, by the day after that, no one was laughing; no one at all. The reason being that one of the most respected figures in town, David Ackert, a prosperous businessman, also encountered the chilling Woman in Black. He noted to newspaper staff that he was six-feet-tall and that, even so, he "had to look up at the woman." It was added that: "*She shrank from him with a hissing sound* [italics mine]." Ackert added, increasing the anxiety around town: "I felt a shivering sensation, for she was so tall and slim and piratical looking."

As fear-levels rose quickly and stratospherically, the local police were determined to put an end to the mystery. The village's four constables – Murray Dederick, Bill Sleight, George Wheeler, and John Heb – vowed to "capture the creature that very night." Unfortunately for everyone, she skilfully avoided the clutches of the police on that night – and also on *every* subsequent night. Next to see the Woman in Black was Thomas Sinclare who, worried readers of the *Herald* were informed: "…was pacing in the middle of the road with her head bent low and her long arms clasped behind her. Sinclare merely took one look." No doubt! Then, one night after that, James Traster, a tinsmith, encountered the village's "mysterious creature" on a side street, around 10:00 p.m. He didn't hang around, either.

It was soon the turn of Florence Welch – "the pretty young teacher at Miller's school" – to see what most were earnestly hoping they would never see. Welch told the newspaper that at around 5:00 p.m., and after leaving a friend's house – that of Mrs. Herman Asher – she happened to walk past the school and saw through a window the WIB sitting on one the student's benches! Wisely, as dusk began to turn to darkness, Florence "ran for her life."

Further reports continued to surface over the next few days, the most notable one being that of Robert Shriver, the village blacksmith. When he saw the WIB he didn't wait for her to hiss malevolently in his direction. What he did was to whip out his pistol and pump three bullets into her. It was all to no avail: the Woman in Black was impervious to the bullets. She raced across nearby, darkened meadows and was lost to the all-enveloping night.

It was to no-one'sno one's satisfaction or comfort that the entire matter remained a disturbing conundrum, as the *Herald* was forced to admit: "Every resident of Rhinebeck is perfectly satisfied that the woman in black is a reality, but not one of them can think of who she can be. There is nobody near here who answers the description of the mysterious creature and there is no family that harbors a crazy person. The nearest asylum is at Poughkeepsie, 16 miles away, and no lunatic has escaped from that institution. To add to the mystery the strange creature is never seen abroad in the daylight and no one has stumbled upon her in any hiding place."

Moving on, let's not forget that in 1952, when Truman Bethurum was hanging out with his WIB from the stars, Aura Rhanes, she hissed malevolently at him in a Nevada diner, during the early hours of a 1952 morning.

```
"Suddenly an eerie hissing noise filled the
interior of the vehicle"
```

Now, let's take a look at the present day. We'll do so with a report prepared by Neil Arnold, who knows a great deal about the matter of the Women in Black and what might appropriately be called their hissy fits. Over to Arnold:

"For almost a century an abundance of motorists while driving through the village of Blue Bell Hill in Kent have claimed to have knocked down, picked up or seen by the roadside a young, forlorn female specter dressed in a pale dress. Over the years the legend has become known as the 'phantom hitchhiker of Blue Bell Hill' and yet what happened during the January of 1993 on that ancient, chalk hill was far more sinister.

"On January 6th at 12:45 a.m. five people – the Maiden family – were traveling in a vehicle up what is known as the Old Chatham Road – the original route through Blue Bell Hill before the construction in the 1970s of the dual carriageway (the A229) – when they observed a figure standing in the road at the edge of the headlight beam. The driver, a Mr. Malcolm Maiden, was accompanied by his wife, Angela, who was the passenger, and in the backseat sat their young daughter who was fast asleep, plus Mrs Maiden's mother and a friend of the family. The figure started across the dark lane; moving from right to left causing Mr Maiden to slow the vehicle. At first, the four witnesses thought that they were being hoaxed by someone in a costume as possibly a very belated Halloween prank. The figure according to Mr Maiden was 'wearing a long old fashioned dress, a tartan shawl round the top and a bonnet with a brim.'

"However, from here things became extremely unnerving. The headlights of the car illuminated a despicable form that appeared to be hunched over 'like when you trap a rabbit in your headlights" but within a split second the apparition had rounded on the vehicle and it was then that the witnesses saw the face. 'It was totally horrific,' Mrs Maiden reported, '[the face was] very small…black beady eyes. It was like a wizened face.' And yet this was not the most terrifying characteristic of the hag.

"'The worst thing of all was the mouth. It opened like an empty black hole. My mother was sitting directly behind me. At the same time I remember we said 'Oh, my God!'

"Suddenly *an eerie hissing noise* filled the interior of the vehicle [italics mine] even though the windows were closed on this cold, clear night. The figure appeared to be clutching a spray of twigs which in a the bony hand, shook aggressively. In panic Mrs. Maiden raised her arm as if to protect herself as the central locking of the car was engaged and finally – breaking from the spell of the hideous entity – Mr. Maiden put the car into correct gear and pulled away from the apparition leaving it to its own devilish devices. Mr.'s Maiden's mother kept her eyes on the figure which seemed to then vanish into the shadows of the treeline and with that Angela's daughter stirred from her slumber; stating that a horrible atmosphere had descended over the vehicle.

"The terrified family told the local newspaper of their ordeal with Mrs. Maiden adding: 'I've never felt evil before and I've never been so terrified. I felt as if I had looked into the eyes of the Devil.'"

"The figure was wearing a long black kind of trench-coat"

Arnold continues: "It could be argued from a sceptical viewpoint that such encounters are rare and most likely involve victims of a clever, albeit disturbing hoax but that is clearly not the case. In 2003 a young couple were travelling up the Old Chatham Road on a dark night when the male driver decided to stop and urinate in the bushes. When he returned to the vehicle he and his girlfriend screamed in terror as a 'witch-like' figure zipped across the dark lane ahead of them. This echoed the case of a lorry driver who in the 1970s was driving up the Chatham Road toward the dual carriageway.

"It was during the early hours on a crisp November when he noticed a hooded figure in black cross the road in the vicinity of the steps which lead down into the woods toward another ancient stone structure named Kits Coty House. On a raining evening just a few years ago a young lady named Miss Hayes was driving home from work heading towards the Lower Bell public house at the bottom of Blue Bell Hill when she noticed through the downpour an old woman in black standing by the roadside. As she approached the motorist observed that the figure was wearing a long black kind of trenchcoat but upon looking again the figure had vanished.

"Rather alarmingly there have been several reports on the hill of an old crone and like in all atmospheric horror stories the encounters nearly always seem to take place on dark, stormy nights during autumn or winter and during the early hours – the witching-hour. Blue Bell Hill is just one of those unique places where not only do ancient stones stand, but many people over the centuries have perished; not just in traffic accidents on that busy A229 but also by other means. But whilst the area has embedded itself into British lore due to its haunting of a young woman in a pale dress; the hag-like apparition has yet to be explained and remains the most disturbing.

"Also in the early 1990s a taxi driver claimed to have seen a witch-like apparition dressed in old-fashioned attire as he travelled on the southbound carriageway during the winter period. He was taking four young men to a night-club in Maidstone when he observed a figure adorned in black standing in undergrowth by the roadside. The figure appeared to be holding some sort of stick and wore a 'long hat' upon its head. According to researcher friend Sean Tudor the youths in the car mocked the figure through the driving rain only for it to vanish!

"And then there was the case of another family who in very similar fashion to the Maiden family encountered a figure at the same spot but in this instant they described an apparition wearing a light-coloured top and holding something akin to lucky heather. The couple were travelling with their two young children on the same road as the Maiden's but the previous night (January 5th 1993) when they drove by the figure. So disturbed were they by the specter that at 3:00 a.m. they telephoned the police at Chatham to report their sighting.

"Women in black are predominant figures in folklore"

"No one is sure as to whether this spectre is some evil old hag or simply the spirit of a gypsy woman or maybe a local recluse who perished years ago, but 'women in black' are predominant figures in folklore. I recall as a child growing up in the Medway Towns close to Blue Bell Hill that many kids would talk about the spectre of an old gypsy-type woman who would travel up the Old Chatham Road via horse and cart – something which would have been quite common in the area a century or so ago – and that she would direct traffic up the hill and then vanish. Other, more imaginative children spoke of a hag in black said to patrol the dark woods, twisted lanes and dual carriageway of Blue Bell Hill accompanied by two formidable ghostly black hounds which she would then unleash onto the road causing vehicles to swerve to avoid them.

"Mind you, I also remember as a child that a local lady would walk the streets of Medway and the surrounding areas dressed in black. She had a white powdered face, light grey hair and was often seen dragging bush along the road. Children were terrified of this very real woman, especially when she would march through a busy town offering dire warnings to those who listened. But one cannot explain as to why there have been so many sightings on the hill over the course of half a century or more.

"Although, coincidentally, I did speak to an elderly fellow a few years ago who told me that in the 1950s he was a fireman and one night he was called out to an old house on the Old Chatham Road after an elderly lady had possibly committed suicide by jumping down the well in her garden. It was his duty of removing her rotten carcass from the water hole. Maybe it's her that haunts the hill. But, then again, there are also records of a rather eccentric old lady residing on the hill and dying of pneumonia back in the 1950s. With a shock of red hair and done up to the nines she would take to the town exuding flamboyance and maybe she still does but in the spectral realm. Even so, with tales of Satanism, witches, hellhounds, giant black cats, mystical stones and a gaggle of ghosts, Blue Bell Hill seems far more active in paranormal terms than say Pluckley in Ashford which has long been touted as Kent's most haunted locale.

"She was always chased by a despicable crone in black"

"However, whilst speaking of Pluckley it's also worth noting a similar hag-like specter which bears some resemblance to the Blue Bell Hill crone. The Watercress Woman is considered one of the twelve (or fourteen!) ghosts said to haunt Pluckley; it is the spirit of an old woman who would sit often sit or collect watercress by the Pinnock Bridge by a nearby stream but who perished after setting herself on fire when she dropped a cigarette/pipe on her alcohol-saturated garments. But then again; these hags are everywhere.

"A few years ago a chap would drive to visit his girl-friend in Lenham at Maidstone because she was often too terrified to drive out of the village because she claimed that she was always chased by a despicable crone in black that would be visible in the rear-view mirror. The hideous apparition would shake a fist – said to be clutching a bunch of sticks – in anger. When I spoke to the man he told me, "I never used to believe my partner until one night we both got in our cars and drove out of her road but as I looked in the rear-view mirror I'm sure I saw the same witch-like crone that she'd reported on several occasions."

"At Boxley Hill, which is just a short journey from Blue Bell Hill there is a very similar setting which takes in the ancient Pilgrims Way path. Boxley Hill is also known for its disturbing apparitions. Although not a hag, what a woman observed around five years ago was still enough to cause her many sleepless nights. She had been driving from Maidstone into the Medway towns via Boxley, Lidsing, etc. when she saw by the roadside a figure she described as looking like a highway man, only his hands were extended in front like he was pleading, or praying. His head was lurched back and she saw his face contorted with horror. According to the witness the figure looked as if it was in pain and distress but its features were also screwed up into an evil sneer with wild gaping eyes and its tongue hanging from its mouth. The figure was adorned in a long coat, and wore 'a funny hat and big boots' and was partly transparent with a greenish hue. The woman sped home in terror but afterwards was plagued by nightmares of the figure."

"They stopped to aid an elderly woman - clad in black - who was standing by the roadside"

"Returning back to the crone we also meet another couple who whilst travelling through Blue Bell Hill around the same time as the Maiden family encountered a figure with 'an old face and blonde hair' and having 'horrible eyes and no lips,' but instead of wearing a cloak it appeared adorned in a kilt. Now, this may sound rather bizarre but in a few encounters with Blue Bell Hill's hag witnesses have reported a tartan pattern of sorts on the shawl. The couple were keen to report their incident to the police who apparently searched the area but could find no sign. The female witness told the local newspaper, 'We (the woman and her husband) turned icy cold…at first we thought it was a man dressed up but now I don't know what it was. It stood on the side of the road and was beckoning us (another feature which seems common in such encounters) with a bunch of heather in its hand but I'm sure it wasn't a gypsy.'

"It has been suggested that the witch-type figure of Blue Bell Hill is not a ghost but some sort of warning appa-rition connected either to the structure of the land or even the psyche of certain, susceptible witnesses. Ten-minutes previous to the recently spoken of encounter, the female witnesses' brother-in-law had travelled the same route and yet did not experience anything untoward. Whilst probably not related, around twenty years ago a relative of mine was driving late at night with his brother along a country lane in Kent when they stopped to aid an elderly woman – clad in black – who was standing by the roadside. However, instead of thanking them for their assistance at such a late hour the figure turned towards the men and in mocking fashion ordered them to 'never cross my path again!'

"Researcher Sean Tudor, who has been investigating the unnatural phenomena attached to Blue Bell Hill since the early '80s commented that, 'Folklore is replete with supernatural characters bearing more than a similarity to the Blue Bell Hill "ghost.' He offers up the legend of Cailleach; found in Celtic and pre-Celtic mythology and which speaks of this "mother goddess" figure said to take on the varying guises of hooded figure or beautiful young woman – also relevant to many sightings on the hill.

"He adds, 'Her depiction is the personification of winter and the triple form of Virgin, Mother and Crone (or Woman Who Devours Men), representing the nurturing and hostile faces of nature and the seasons' which certainly bear relevance to the encounters and periods of such events on the hill. It could also be argued that in spite of its terrible appearance; the 'hag' is merely a guardian appearing as it does to warn people of a coming danger. Maybe it takes such a hideous form to prevent speeding motorists from taking a sharp bend too quickly and throughout folklore there are mentions of similar manifestations appearing during tragedies and disasters."

"One only has to look at the 'woman in black' in folklore to realize how potent a form it is"

"It's fair to say that witches and old women seemingly of that ilk have plagued our thoughts for many years. Could it be possible that a handful of centuries ago and up until the 19th century, a reclusive old woman or two were to be taken to somewhere - such as Penenden Heath - in nearby Maidstone and executed for being a witch? This was certainly a common practice not so long ago; it is recorded that in 1652 'Anne Ashby, alias Cobler, Anne Martyn, Mary Browne, Anne Wilson, and Mildred Wright of Cranbrook, and Mary Read, of Lenham, being legally convicted, were according to the Laws of this Nation, adjudged to be hanged, at the common place of Execution. Some there were that wished rather, they might be burnt to Ashes; alleging that it was a received opinion among many, that the body of a witch being burnt, her bloud is prevented thereby from becoming [sic] hereditary to her Progeny in the same evil'.

"Some alleged practitioners of 'witchcraft' were thought to have been interred at unmarked graves (after being hanged at Maidstone) dotted throughout Kent or their skeletons beheaded and in some instances staked before their remains were buried at old crossroads. Blue Bell Hill has at least two ancient crossroads where many deaths have taken place over the years. But one only has to look at the 'woman in black' in folklore to realise how potent a form it is and 'witchcraft' was certainly rife in Kent; or at least the fear of it was. For example, in 1586 a Joan Cason was accused, via 'witchcraft', of killing a child named Joan Crook. She was tried at Faversham and accused of having 'familiars. She was sentenced to death. The year 1671 saw a Woolwich widow tried in

Kent for feeding, entertaining and employing a familiar that looked like a rat. Whilst in 1692 three women were accused of consulting and covenanting with strange creatures in the shape of mice. But why so many spectres should gather on Blue Bell Hill is something we will never know; and yet such spectres and of similar guise or purpose are recorded everywhere.

"In the village of Highgate in north London people have had encounters with a shadowy male figure said to appear by the roadside of Swains Lane or on some occasions hitch a lift or even *hiss at those frequenting the area* [italics mine]. Stranger still, she also reports on numerous other darkly clad, cowled entities in the area known to frighten motorists with one witnesses claiming that the male specter they saw was 'full of evil.' And yet within paranormal realms researchers often state that there is no such thing as coincidence, and so with that I also must mention the 'mad old woman' searching among the graves that Mrs. Farrant also writes of. She adds that a decrepit specter was once believed to have roamed Highgate Cemetery in search of her children which were buried there – this being another common theme in ghost lore, but what is odd is the mention of a Maiden Lane in the vicinity of the alleged haunting; again reverting as back to the triple goddess connections.

"And lastly, but of a more prosaic quality, *The Morning Herald* of December 9th 1887 reported, 'The Ghost Found – And It Turns Out To Be A Poor Demented Woman', after reports in Atlanta, Georgia of a mysterious woman in black had plagued local residents. The woman, said to have a pale face 'now and then appeared on a trestle on the belt road, near where it crosses the Georgia Pacific.'

"According to local railroad workers every time the woman appeared a terrible disaster would take place and when anyone dared approach the woman she would simply vanish. Some people believed the sinister wraith to be a witch, but according to the newspaper, 'Friday morning the 'ghost' was found lying in a pool of water unconscious and nearly frozen to death…the woman was evidently not sane.'

"The woman claimed her name was Annie Garrett and that she had become disgusted with the world and so decided to go and live in the woods – hence her dishevelled appearance. Her ability to seemingly vanish when people approached was explained by a hole under the trestle in which she had probably slept. But the next time you're driving through Blue Bell Hill, or on any country road, for that matter, always stay alert because during the season of the witch anything is possible."

26

"The woods are
avoided after dusk"

In 2015, I dug deep into a wave of WIB/UFO activity that occurred in the first decade of the 20th century, and which reached its pinnacle just before the decade came to its close. In 1909, the U.K. was hit by a strange wave of largely nighttime encounters with what can only be termed UFOs. Particularly hard hit by the mysterious, aerial intruders was Wales. Brett Holman, who has extensively studied this issue, says:

"On the night of 23 March 1909, a police constable named Kettle saw a most unusual thing: 'a strange, cigar-shaped craft passing over the city of Peterborough, Cambridgeshire. His friends were skeptical, but his story was corroborated, to an extent, by Mr Banyard and Mrs Day, both of nearby March, who separately saw something similar two nights later. In fact, these incidents were only the prelude to a series of several dozen such sightings throughout April and especially May, mostly from East Anglia and South Wales."

In May of the same year, the *London Standard* newspaper told its readers that with "few exceptions" the witnesses described seeing "a torpedo-shaped object, possessing two powerful searchlights, which comes out early at night."

A "phantom airship" of the mysterious kind.
(San Francisco Call, 1896).

Holman continues: "So, what was torpedo-shaped and capable of flight in 1909? An airship, of course. The press (metropolitan and provincial) certainly assumed that the most likely explanation for these 'fly-by-nights' was an airship or airships, generally terming them 'phantom airships,' 'mystery airships,' 'scareships' or something similar. But whose airship? Where was it from?" They were, and still are, important questions.

The prevailing theory – hysteria aside – was that the airships were the creations of the Germans, secretly scanning the U.K. by night. Maybe that was the case. It's intriguing to note, however, that there were more than a few Women in Black and MIB encounters in this period. It's worth noting, too, that some of the reports do indeed have a distinct air of the UFO attached to them.

"They attracted my close attention because of their peculiar getup"

May 18, 1909 was the night on which one of the most amazing encounters occurred. A Mr. C. Lethbridge was walking to his Roland Street, Cardiff home, via the 271-meter-high Caerphilly Mountain. As he did so, Lethbridge was astonished by the sight of a cigar-shaped vehicle – in excess of forty-feet in length – which was sitting on the grass, at the edge of a mountain road. In his very own words…

"When I turned the bend at the summit I was surprised

to see a long tube-shaped affair on the grass on the roadside, with two men busily engaged with something nearby. They attracted my close attention because of their peculiar getup; they appeared to have big heavy fur coats and fur caps fitting tightly over their heads. I was rather frightened, but I continued to go on until I was within twenty yards of them, and then my idea as to their clothing was confirmed.

"The noise of my little spring cart seemed to attract them, and when they saw me they jumped up and jabbered furiously to each other in a strange lingo — Welsh or something else; it was certainly not English. They hurriedly collected something off the ground, and then I was really frightened. The long thing on the ground rose up slowly. I was standing still at the time, quite amazed, and when it was hanging a few feet off the ground the men jumped into a kind of little carriage suspended from it, and gradually the whole affair and the men rose in the air in a zigzag fashion. When they had cleared the telegraph wires that pass over the mountain, two lights like electric lamps shone out, and the thing went higher into the air, and sailed away towards Cardiff."

It appears that although the mysterious airships surfaced in 1909, the story actually dates back to 1905.

"This figure has delivered a message"

Ray Boeche, of Lincoln, Nebraska, is an Anglican priest and a former state-director for the Mutual UFO Network:

MUFON. A firm believer in the existence of the UFO phenomenon, Boeche does not believe it has extraterrestrial origins. Rather, his conclusion is that the phenomenon is demonic – and that includes the dark-suited figures we have come to know so well. Boeche says:

"The Welsh airship flap of 1909 resulted in many MIB-like encounters, the mysterious visitors usually reported to have been speaking in some strange, unknown language. An event from four years earlier, in 1905, may be even more interesting. During the spring of that year, Wales was inundated with sightings of mysterious aerial lights. On March 30, 1905, the *Barmouth Advertiser* carried this item: 'In the neighborhood dwells an exceptionally intelligent young woman of the peasant stock, whose bedroom has been visited three nights in succession by a man dressed in black. This figure has delivered a message to the girl which she is too frightened to relate.' It is interesting to note that this event comes in the midst of the great Welsh Christian revival of 1904-05."

"He saw a lady in black enter his bedroom"

It's equally interesting to note that in March 1905 a story surfaced in the pages of the *Cambrian*, which was the very first Welsh newspaper and which opened for business in 1804. The March 3, 1905 edition included a small article titled "Lampeter Ghost: 'Lady in Black.'" Lampeter is a town in southwest Wales, the origins of which date back to the 12th century. The article reads as follows:

"The Lampeter ghost has now assumed, or rather is credited, with a dual personality. It is stated that the restless spirits are those of a man and wife. Latest testimony from Lampeter is to the effect that as late as Wednesday morning ghostly footsteps were heard ascending and descending the stairs. The boy Jack has declared that he saw a lady in black enter his bedroom and leave it, noiselessly closing it.

"The servant Jane has heard mysterious 'calls' from one of the troubled 'spooks' in the corridor, the sound partaking of a curious humming noise, as though the spirit had some message to communicate, but was unable to.

"Mrs. Howell, be it stated, is a woman whom no one for a moment suspects as being of the stamp to regale her friends with fictitious narrations, and there is an old woman now in the neighborhood who declares that years ago when in service with another family in the same house she heard similar manifestations, so that the whole affair is a thoroughly weird and uncanny one.

"As if in celebration of St. David's Day, the ghosts kept banging kitchen chairs about until the inhabitants left the room in terror."

"She seemed to have a slight stoop, and was
dressed in black"

"Good folk at Birkenhead are puzzled about weird and ghostly phenomena that have occurred on the Woodchurch Road." That was the opening line in an article that appeared in the *Evening Express* on April 29, 1905.

One witness told the newspaper: "I have frequently met at night, at different hours, what appeared to be an elderly lady, right in front of my bicycle, and on two occasions lately was compelled to apply the brakes suddenly to avert a collision. Invariably in each case has been only momentarily, the old lady vanishing into the darkness. She seemed to have a slight stoop, and was dressed in black, with a grey shawl and grey bonnet."

The *Evening Express* noted: "A few years ago, in the neighborhood where the apparition is now seen, an old lady left her house to go for what was her customary walk, but from that time to this she has never been heard of."

And reports continued across the U.K. throughout the years that followed.

"A black figure with one white arm and a
white leg"

Moving onto October 4, 1906, the *Evening Express* revealed that there was a "black and white ghost" of terrifying proportions on the loose in "Lonesome, the deserted village near Mitcham Common." The tale continued like this: the ghost in black "…terrorizes the inhabitants of the neighboring districts. A row of villas was partly built, near the woods at Mitcham, twenty years ago, and then the work was suddenly abandoned. The place is known as the deserted village. It is in the buildings and on a tortuous path between the villas and the woods that people assert the ghost appears."

One of those people, the *Express* said, was a man who worked at "Polloks Hill brickfield." He was willing to share the details of his unnerving encounter, which went as follows:

"As I was crossing by the woods, I heard a piercing shriek, and then saw in the distance a black figure with one white arm and a white leg. I followed it, and it again shrieked and appeared to drop through the ground. I ran to the spot, but before reaching it the thing rose and, again shrieking, glided over the ground and entered the barn. The door was banged to, and then such a fearful row inside ensued that I was scared and came away."

"The woods are avoided after dusk"

- -

Under the heading of "A Cheshire Ghost Story," on November 7, 1907, the *Evening Express* told its readers: "A sensation has been occasioned at the village of Barnton, Northwich, by what is designated a 'veiled lady.' It is declared that late at night and during the small hours of the morning, an apparition in black, wearing a thick veil, has been seen parading certain roads. The superstitious are quite alarmed, but it is suggested that the ghost is the trick of a practical joker or some person mentally deranged. The ghost disappears suddenly across fields on the appearance of pedestrians."

The article was concluded in appropriately nerve-jangling fashion: "Other people tell similar tales, and all Lonesome and the woods are avoided after dusk."

"A lady dressed in the deepest black"

"Ghostly Visitant" was the headline that jumped out of the pages of the *Evening Express* on November 28, 1908. Its undoubtedly worried readers: "Woodstone, a suburb of Peterborough, is said to have a ghostly visitant, and many of the inhabitants are terror-stricken. The first to claim to have seen the apparition was a woman, who was passing along a lonely path near the churchyard at dusk and says she met 'a lady dressed in the deepest black,'" and stood aside for her to pass. With a rustle of her gown, however, the figure vanished, and the woman ran away shrieking. Other people who allege that they have seen the somber figure say it has a ghastly white face, and that its hands are outstretched. Parties of 'watchers' are being organized to 'lay the spirit.'"

"The Village Ghost" was the title of a small news item that appeared in the *Evening Express*. According to the

unknown writer of the feature: "Not a little commotion has
been created among the inhabitants of the wayside village of
Osgodby, near Selby, by the strange appearance of a noctur-
nal visitor, which some people describe as a 'ghost.' On one
occasion the apparition is said to have stepped in front of a
horse and trap belonging to a local farmer, and after saying
'Goodnight' in sepulchered tones disappeared into the trees
nearby. On another occasion, when a passing cyclist seemed
to run into it, the ghost was clothed in female attire, with a
black veil over her face."

All of which brings us back to 1909 and the Women
in Black.

"Woman In Black Again In Town"

On January 30, 1909, the Wales-based *Cardiff Times* newspaper ran a news-story titled "Black Ghost." The story told
of how "two laborers," Benjamin Benns and Robert Elvin
– both of Beccles, England – encountered a ghostly figure in
the vicinity of Roos Hall on the evening of January 18, 1909.
Elvin, however, had a previous encounter: approximately
a week before Christmas 1908. The ghost was described
as "about 5ft. 9in. in height, with nice-cut features, like a
woman," and was of a "very black, shadowy appearance."

Then, on November 20, 1909, Wales' *Prestatyn Weekly*
told of the antics of a "young woman dressed in black who
had been busy stealing various and sundry items from homes

in the Prestatyn region. The article was titled "The Woman in Black."

Nine days later, in Gettysburg, United States, the local newspaper – the *Gettysburg Times* – included an article in its pages titled "Woman In Black Again In Town." The sub-title read: "Mysterious Character again Appears in North End of Town, Peering into Windows and Alarming Women." Those that encountered the woman, noted the media, said she stood a couple of inches short of six-feet and wore "a heavy black veil and a black dress."

As all of the above shows, the first decade of the 20th century was filled to the brim with accounts of our now-familiar Women in Black. It was, as we have also seen, a decade noted for its intriguing UFO encounters. Coincidence? Most unlikely.

Conclusions

Our story is now at its end. And a bizarre and disturbing story it has certainly been. As I mentioned in the Introduction to this book, within the field of Ufology, the matter of the Women in Black has largely gone by unnoticed and / or unappreciated. Until now, that is. As we have seen in the previous pages, and time and time again, the WIB have been at the forefront of absolutely numerous encounters of the UFO and paranormal variety.

From the 19th to the 21st century, these fear-inducing females showed a chilling predilection for trying to kidnap babies and young children. In the 1930s, a particularly dangerous WIB plagued the Bender family of Bridgeport, Connecticut – a family which was inextricably tied to the riddle of the Men in Black. A famous Contactee of the 1950s – Truman Bethurum – became utterly entranced and enchanted by one of these deceptive things. A high-ranking figure in the British military had an intimidating, face-to-face meeting with a pale-skinned Woman in Black in the mid-fifties. When the red-eyed, winged beast known as Mothman manifested in Point Pleasant, West Virginia in the 1960s, the WIB were quickly on the scene, posing as census-takers and gypsies. One of this deadly breed may have tried to infiltrate the heart of the Nixon administration in the early 1970s. They surfaced from their darkened lairs when, in 1987, Whitley Strieber's best-selling book, *Communion*, was published. We've seen them plunge people into deep states of terror, anxiety, and unrelenting paranoia. The saga of Colin Perks, of 2000, and his King Arthur-themed research is a perfect, and ultimately fatal, example of that. And then there are the latter-day confrontations with truly disturbing Women in Black, such as those encountered by Denise Stoner, Christina George, and "A Hesitant Believer."

So, who, exactly, are the Women in Black? Just like their close compatriots, the Men in Black, it's abundantly clear they're not the employees of any agency of government, the military, or the intelligence community. Such is very much the imagery played out in the likes of the *Men in Black* movie franchise. The fact is, however, that the WIB are, simply put, just too strange to be anything as down-to-earth as "secret agents." From the Pentagon, they're not. That we see, time and again, the Women in Black tied to cases with paranormal, and even demonic, overtones, is a good indicator that whatever their points of origin, the NSA and the CIA are certainly not among them, either.

This provokes an important question: if the WIB do have supernatural origins, then what does that say about the overall UFO phenomenon they are so tied to? Should we consider it, too, to be of paranormal – rather than extraterrestrial – origins? Yes, almost certainly: acclaimed researcher-writers such as Jacques Vallee and the late John Keel noted the undeniable parallels between Ufology and numerous other supernatural activity. Unfortunately, they were very much lone wolves; the majority of Ufology preferring to stay snug and safe in their world of "nuts and bolts" Ufology.

As this book has shown, however, there is nothing snug or safe about Ufology. Quite the opposite, actually: it is a domain filled with fear, menace, ruined and wrecked lives, and occult overtones. And, it's a realm overflowing with the Women in Black, too. Whether they are time-travelers, extraterrestrials, half-human and half-alien hybrids, demonic entities, cryptoterrestrials, or, even, a combination of more than one phenomena, of only two things can we be certain: the Women in Black are a reality, and they are here to stay. Neither fact is comforting. Both, however, are terrifying.

Watch out for the Women in Black
(Zachary P. Humway, 2016).

Bibliography

"A Black And White Ghost!" *Evening Express*, October 4, 1906.

"A Cheshire Ghost Story." *Evening Express*, November 7, 1907.

"A Woman In Black." *Sunday Herald*, January 13, 1893.

"A Woman In Black: Arrested And Discharged." *Portsmouth Evening News*, December 15, 1894.

"Apol and Agar." http://www.johnkeel.com/?p=898. October 21, 2011.

Arnold, Neil. "The Blue Bell Hill Project, Part-1: Season of the Witch." 2014.

Arnold, Neil. "The Woman in Black." 2011.

"Assorted Minor MIB Encounters." http://thenightsky.org/mib1.html. January 12, 2016.

Barker, Gray. *M.I.B.: The Secret Terror Among Us*. Clarksburg, WV, New Age Press, 1983.

Barker, Gray. *The Silver Bridge*. Clarksburg, W.V., Saucerian Books, 1970.

Barker, Gray. *They Knew Too Much About Flying Saucers*. NY, University Books, Inc., 1956.

Beckley, Timothy Green and Stuart, John. *Curse of the Men in Black*. New Brunswick, NJ, Global Communications, 2010.

Beckley, Timothy Green. *The UFO Silencers (Special Edition)*. New Brunswick, NJ, Inner Light Publications, 1990.

Bender, Albert. *Flying Saucers and the Three Men*. NY, Paperback Library, Inc., 1968.

Bennett-Smith, Meredith. "Mystery Of 1938 'Time Traveler' With Cell Phone Solved? (VIDEO)?"

http://www.huffingtonpost.com/2013/04/04/time-traveler-cell-phone-1938-video-woman-factory_n_3013996.html. April 4, 2013.

Bethurum, Truman. *Aboard a Flying Saucer*. Los Angeles, CA, DeVorss & Co., 1955.

Bethurum, Truman. *The Voice of the Planet Clarion*, self-published, 1957.

Bethurum, Truman and Beckley, Timothy Green. *The People of the Planet Clarion*. Clarksburg, WV, Saucerian Books, 1970.

"Black Ghost." *Cardiff Times*, January 30, 1909.

"Blamed on Hypnosis." *Sarasota Journal*, October 22, 1971.

"Bogus Social Workers Hunt." *Scottish Daily Record*, October 21, 2001.

Boeche, Raymond W. *Caught in a Web of Deception*. University of Nebraska Press, Lincoln, NE, 1994.

"Chaplin's Time Traveler." https://www.youtube.com/watch?v=Y6a4T2tJaSU. October 19, 2010.

Clarke, Dr. David and Roberts, Andy. *Out of the Shadows*. London, U.K., Piatkus, 2002.

Colvin, Andrew B. *The Mothman's Photographer II*. Seattle, WA, MetaDiscs Books, 2007.

Conroy, Ed. *Report on Communion*. NY, Avon Books, 1989.

Crabb, Riley. "Gray Barker's latest Flying Saucer book, reviewed by the Editor, Riley Crabb." *Journal of Borderland Research*, Vol. 18, No. 8. https://borderlandsciences.org/journal/vol/18/n08/Crabb_on_Bender_Three_Men_I.html. 2015.

Criscione, Arthur. "Mount Misery and Sweet Hollow Road." http://weirdus.com/states/new_york/road_less_traveled/mount_misery_road/index.php. 2015.

Crowther, Linnea. "Jeane Dixon's Prophecies." http://www.legacy.com/news/celebrity-deaths/article/jeane-dixons-prophecies. 2011.

Dash, Mike. *Borderlands, The Ultimate Exploration of the Unknown*. NY, Dell Publishing, 2000.

DeBarra, Damien. "Prophecies Fulfilled." http://www.blather.net/theblather/1998/06/prophecies_fulfilled/. June 19, 1998.

Decker, Nathan and Burda, Pam. "Devil Girl from Mars (1954)." http://www.millionmonkeytheater.com/DevilGirlMars.html. April 2012.

Doc Conjure. "Hyre, Mary." http://thedemoniacal.blogspot.com/2009/07/hyre-mary.html. July 6, 2009.

Doc Conjure. "Police Officer Attacked By Flying Witch."

http://thedemoniacal.blogspot.com/2009/05/police-officer-attacked-by-flying-witch.html. May 31, 2009.

Downes, Jonathan and Wright, Nigel. *The Rising of the Moon*. Bangor, Northern Ireland, Xiphos Books, 2005.

Dr. Abner Mality. "Phantom Clowns." http://www.wormwoodchronicles.net/wormwood-files/phantom-clowns. 2015.

"Dr. Herbert Hopkins." http://realmib.tripod.com/hopkins.html. 2015.

Felix. Email to Nick Redfern, November 24, 2015.

Firth, Niall. "Is this a time-traveler in a Charlie Chaplin film? Footage from 1928 shows woman 'using a mobile phone.'" http://www.dailymail.co.uk/sciencetech/article-1324132/Time-traveller-woman-mobile-phone-1928-Charlie-Chaplin-film.html. November 1, 2010.

Gayle, Damien. "Police hunt for bogus social worker after woman examines new mother's baby by showing false ID badge to gain entry to their home." http://www.dailymail.co.uk/news/article-2613393/Police-hunt-bogus-social-worker-woman-examines-new-mothers-baby-showing-false-ID-badge-gain-entry-home.html. April 26, 2014.

Gerhard, Ken. *Encounters with Flying Humanoids*. Woodbury, MN, Llewellyn Publications, 2013.

Gerhard, Ken and Redfern, Nick. *Monsters of Texas*. Woolsery, U.K., CFZ Press, 2010.

"Ghost of 'Lady in Black' Still Haunts Fort Warren Troops." *Milwaukee Journal*, October 17, 1941.

"'Ghost' Seen On Bridge: Mysterious Woman in Black Cloak Puzzles Town." *Reading Eagle*. March 2, 1953.

"Ghostly Visitant." *Evening Express*, November 28, 1908.

"Gliding Ghost." *Gloucester Citizen*, December 23, 1921.

Good, Timothy. *Alien Base*. London, U.K., Random House, 1998.

Hall, Manly P. *The Secret Teachings of all Ages*. Radford, VA, Wilder Publications, 2009.

Harpur, Damien. *Daimonic Reality*. Ravensdale, WA, Pine Winds Press, 2003.

Harpur, Merrily. *Mystery Big Cats*. Avebury, U.K., Heart of Albion Press, 2006.

Harney, John. "Should 'Men in Black' reports be taken seriously?" *Merseyside UFO Bulletin*, no. 5, September-October 1968.

"He Saw 'The Black Lady.'" *Sunday Post*, January 1, 1950.

"Hearing Aid." http://hearraid.com/page/325/. 2015.

Hollis, Heidi. *The Hat Man*. Milwaukee, WI, Level Head
Publishing, 2014.

Holman, Brett. "The Scareship Age." http://airminded.
org/2006/12/22/the-scareship-age/. December 22, 2006.

Homren, Wayne. "More on the Alchemical Medallion."

http://www.coinbooks.org/esylum_v13n52a12.html.

Hopkins, Budd. *Intruders*. NY, Ballantine Books, 1997.

Horsley, Peter. *Sounds from Another Room*. Barnsley, U.K., Pen and
Sword Books, 1998.

House of Commons. http://www.publications.parliament.uk/pa/
cm199798/cmhansrd/vo980202/debtext/80202-35.htm.
February 2, 1998.

"Influence Of Alchemy In Frankenstein, English Literature Essay."
http://www.ukessays.com/essays/english-literature/influence-of-
alchemy-in-frankenstein-english-literature-essay.php.2015.

"Invasion Scares – Queer Stories from Humberside." *Exmouth Journal*,
May 21, 1909.

"Is this the world's first cell phone? Film from 1938 shows a woman
talking on a wireless device… but it is not 'time travel' family say to
the disappointment of conspiracy theorists." http://www.dailymail.
co.uk/news/article-2301996/Was-worlds-mobile-phone-1938-
film-shows-woman-talking-wireless-device-time-travel-family-say-
disappointment-conspiracy-theorists.html. April 3, 2013.

Jacobs, David M. *Walking Among Us*. NY, Disinformation Books, 2015.

"Jaye P. Paro – and the Mount Misery Photo." http://www.johnkeel.
com/?p=246. March 18, 2010.

Keith, Jim. *Casebook of the Men in Black*. Lilburn, GA, IllumiNet Press, 1997.

Keel, John A. "Mysterious Voices From Outer Space." *UFO Report 2*, no. 6, Winter 1975.

Keel, John A. *Operation Trojan Horse*. London, U.K., Souvenir Press, Ltd., 1971.

Keel, John A. *Our Haunted Planet*. London, U.K., Futura Publications, Ltd., 1971.

Keel, John. "Problems of Identity: The Aliens Among Us." *Saga UFO Report*, 1977.

Keel, John A. *The Complete Guide to Mysterious Beings*. NY, Tor Books, 2002.

Keel, John A. *The Mothman Prophecies*. NY, Tor Books, 1991.

Keel, John A. "The Strange Case of the Pregnant Woman." *Searching for the String: Selected Writings of John Keel*. Seattle, WA, Metadisc Productions, Seatle, WA, 2014.

Kopun, Francine. "Does mummified baby have living cousin?" http://www.thestar.com/news/gta/2007/09/24/does_mummified_baby_have_living_cousin.html. September 24, 2007.

"Lampeter Ghost: 'Lady in Black." *The Cambrian*, March 3, 1905.

"Large alchemical medallion by Johann Wenzel Seiler, 1672." 2015.

Levi St. Armand, Barton. "Poe's 'Sober Mystification.'" *Poe Studies*, Vol. 4, No. 1, 1971.

Levi St. Armand, Barton. "Usher Unveiled: Poe and the Metaphysic of Gnosticism." *Poe Studies*, Vol. 5, No. 1, June 1972.

"Lia and Company." http://www.johnkeel.com/?p=893. October 20, 2011.

Linsboth, Christina. "Turning lead into silver – Experiments in alchemy at the Imperial Court." http://www.habsburger.net/en/chapter/turning-lead-silver-experiments-alchemy-imperial-court. 2015

Lovecraft, H.P. "The Alchemist." *The United Amateur*, November 1916.

Mackay, Charles. *Extraordinary Popular Delusions*. NY, Dover Publications, 2003.

"Mary Hyre's Obituary." http://www.johnkeel.com/?p=220. February 17, 2010.

Medway, Gareth J. "Men in Black Encounters, a Short Catalogue." http://pelicanist.blogspot.com/p/mib-encounters.html. 2015.

Meehan, Paul. "Phantom Clowns, Bogus Social Workers, and Men in Black." http://www.theofantastique.com/2011/11/30/phantom-clowns-bogus-social-workers-and-men-in-black/. November 30, 2011.

Moonlight, a.k.a. Amanda. "The Gwrach y Rhibyn." http://www.vampires.com/the-gwrach-y-rhibyn/. July 11, 2010.

Mulligan, Colin. "The Great British Scareship Mystery of 1909." http://www.ufocasebook.com/scareship1909.html. 2015.

Murray, Frank. "Saga of the Men in Black." *Beyond Reality*, no, 18, January 1976.

"Mysterious Lady in Black." *Evening Express*, May 16, 1910.

Newman, F.B. "Who are the 'Men in Black?'" *UFO Magazine*, no. 1, March 1978.

"Nixon Maid Stole In Trance, She Says." *Washington Post*, October 23, 1971.

Offutt, Jason. *Darkness Walks*. San Antonio, TX, Anomalist Books, 2009.

Randles, Jenny. *MIB: Investigating the Truth Behind the Men in Black Phenomenon*, Piatkus, London, U.K., 1997.

Redfern, Nick. *Chupacabra Road Trip*. Woodbury, MN, Llewelyn Publications, 2015.

Redfern, Nick. *Men in Black: Personal Stories & Eerie Adventures.* Lisa Hagan Books, VA., 2015.

Redfern, Nick. *On the Trail of the Saucer Spies*. San Antonio, TX, Anomalist Books, 2006.

Redfern, Nick. *The Real Men in Black*. Pompton Plains, NJ, New Page Books, 2011.

Reynolds, Rich. "When the Men in Black were once the Men in White." http://ufocon.blogspot.com/2012_07_31_archive.html. July 31, 2012.

Rogerson, Peter. "Somewhere a Child is Crying." *Magonia*, No. 38, 1991.

Rojcewicz, Peter M. "The 'Men in Black' Experience and Tradition: Analogues with the Traditional Devil Hypothesis." *The Journal of American Folklore*, no. 396, April-June 1987.

Schwarz, Berthold. "The Man in Black Syndrome." *Flying Saucer Review*, Vol. 23, No. 4, 1977.

Schwarz, Berthold. *UFO Dynamics*. Moore Haven, FL, Rainbow Books, 1988.

Sikes, Wirt. *British Goblins*. London, U.K., Sampson Low, 1880.

Steiger, Brad. "Ancient Secret Societies, UFOs, and the New World Order." http://www.bibliotecapleyades.net/sociopolitica/sociopol_brotherhoodss30.htm. January 29, 2008.

Steiger, Brad. "Three Tricksters in Black." *Saga's UFO Report*, winter 1974.

Stebner, Beth. "The most dangerous drug in the world: 'Devil's Breath' chemical from Colombia can block free will, wipe memory and even kill." http://www.dailymail.co.uk/news/article-2143584/Scopolamine-Powerful-drug-growing-forests-Colombia-ELIMINATES-free-will.html. May 12, 2012.

Strieber, Whitley. *Communion*. NY, William Morrow, 1987.

Strieber, Whitley. Transformation. NY, William Morrow, 1988.

"The Lady In Black." *Weekly Mail*, October 31, 1891.

"The Philosopher's Stone." http://montalk.net/gnosis/174/the-philosopher-s-stone. 2015.

"The Strange Case of the Pregnant Woman (1)." http://www.johnkeel.com/?p=1968. July 17, 2013.

"The Strange Case of the Pregnant Woman (2)." http://www.johnkeel.com/?p=1976. July 19, 2013.

"The Strange Case of the Pregnant Woman (3)." http://www.johnkeel.com/?p=1985. July 23, 2013.

"The Strange Case of the Pregnant Woman (4)." http://www.johnkeel.com/?p=1994. July 30, 2013.

"The Strange Case of the Pregnant Woman (5)." http://www.johnkeel.com/?p=2002. August 6, 2013.

"The Strange Case of the Pregnant Woman (6). http://www.johnkeel.com/?p=2009. August 12, 2013.

"The Village Ghost." *Evening Express*, November 3, 1910.

"The Woman In Black – A Queer Character That Is Causing A Sensation In Scranton (Pennsylvania)." *New York Times*, November 10, 1886.

"The Woman in Black: Incident at the House of Mr. Rupert Guiness." *Nottingham Evening Post*, November 29, 1912.

"The Woman in Black: Pauper Child Kidnapped." *Evening Post*, January 2, 1909.

"The Woman in Black." *Prestatyn Weekly*, November 20, 1909.

"The Woman in Black." *Sunday Herald*, January 17, 1898.

"Time Traveler Caught on Film - Time Traveler Cell Phone - Charlie Chaplin Time Traveler."

https://www.youtube.com/watch?v=TiIrpEMbQ2M. October 27, 2010.

Tonnies, Mac. *The Cryptoterrestrials*. San Antonio, TX, Anomalist Books, 2010.

Totten, Karen. "Encounters." http://postreason.blogspot.com/2009/03/encounters.html. March 25, 2009.

Trevelyan, Mary. *Folk-Lore and Folk-Stories of Wales*. Elliott Stock, London, U.K., 1909.

"Vanishing Lady's Ghost." *Evening Express*, April 29, 1905.

Velez, John. "Police Officer Attacked By Flying Humanoid In Monterrey, Mexico." http://ufocasebook.com/flyinghumanoid.html. 2015.

Warren Larry & Robbins, Peter. NY, *Left at East Gate*, Cosimo, 2005.

Weatherly, David. *The Black Eyed Children*. AZ, Leprechaun Press, 2012.

Wells, Jeff. "Phantoms, Daemons and Finders." http://
rigorousintuition.blogspot.com/2005/10/phantoms-daemons-and-
finders.html. October 13, 2005.

"Western Electric Model 34A 'Audiphone' Carbon Hearing Aid."
http://www.hearingaidmuseum.com/gallery/Carbon/WesternElectric/
info/westelect34a.htm. 2015.

"Woman in Black." *Daily Mail and Empire*, April 7, 1898.

"Woman in Black." *Evening Express*, May 11, 1903.

"Woman in Black Again in Town." *Gettysburg Times*,
November 29, 1909.

Worley, Don. "The Winged Lady in Black." *Flying Saucer Review, Case
Histories*, no. 10, June 1972.

X, Ryan. "John Keel and His Adventures into Unreality." http://
www.sott.net/article/229112-John-Keel-and-His-Adventures-into-
Unreality. May 25, 2011.

About Nick Redfern

Nick Redfern is the author of 36 books on UFOs, lake-monsters, the Roswell UFO crash, zombies, and Hollywood scandal, including *Men in Black*; *Chupacabra Road Trip*; *The Bigfoot Book*; and *Close Encounters of the Fatal Kind*. Nick has appeared on many TV shows, including: Fox News; the BBC's *Out of This World*; the SyFy Channel's *Proof Positive*; the History Channel's *Monster Quest*, *America's Book of Secrets*, *Ancient Aliens* and *UFO Hunters*; the National Geographic Channel's *Paranatural*; and MSNBC's *Countdown with Keith Olbermann*. He can be contacted at: http:// nickredfernfortean.blogspot.com

Acknowledgments

I would like to offer my very sincere thanks to all of the following: my literary agent, publisher and friend, Lisa Hagan; my editor and co-publisher, Beth Wareham; book-designer, Simon Hartshorne; good mate Neil Arnold, for providing me his voluminous body of material on 19th century Women in Black; Zachary P. Humway, for his outstanding artwork; Christina George, who generously shared her time and experiences with me; Karen Totten, for her personal story of the creepy kind; Nigel Wright, long-time friend and researcher; Denise Stoner, a tireless truth-seeker; and "A Hesitant Believer," for taking the time to relate his experiences with both a WIB and a MIB. Thanks!